A Geometry of Lilies

A Geometry of Lilies

Life and Death in an American Family

Steven Harvey

University of South Carolina Press

Copyright © 1993 University of South Carolina

Published in Columbia, South Carolina, by the
University of South Carolina Press

Manufactured in the United States of America

Library of Congress Cataloging-in-Publication Data

Harvey, Steven, 1949 June 9–
    A geometry of lilies : life and death in an American family /
Steven Harvey.
        p.   cm.
    Contents: The nuclear family — Kid talk — The eternal seventh
grade — Endless imitation — Unheard melodies — Furnished rooms —
The old surprises — The garden wall — Suicide notes — Monogamy —
The geometry of lilies.
    ISBN 0–87249–895–6 (hard cover : acid-free)
    1. Harvey, Steven, 1949 June 9– —Family.   2. Authors,
American—20th century—Biography.   3. Family—United States.
I. Title.
PS3558.A7195Z467   1993
818'.5409—dc20
    [B]   93-1349
                                                                  CIP

To Matt, Nessa, Sam, Alice, and,
above all, Barbara—my nuclear family.

Consider the lilies of the field, how they grow.
—Matthew

God is a geometer.
—Plato

Contents

A Geometry of Lilies

Prologue

Out of nowhere they appear! The little ones pull on my arms, nearly spilling my drink, and the older girl climbs up on the sofa and sits on my shoulders, legs straddling my neck. "Wrestle! Wrestle! Let's wrestle Daddy."

I shake them off, setting down the glass and shedding my jacket. The game begins.

I marvel at the transparent guile of their planning huddles, the determined looks as they gather courage for the synchronized assault, their reckless confidence as they throw their bodies at their father. I'm deceived by the ease with which I can turn aside the little attackers, taking a fatherly pride in lifting them high, bringing their screaming bodies down safely, and turning hurts into giggles with tickling. Wrestling like this pleases us all. It's illusion, papa magic, the fatherly art of making soft landings out of imagined dangers. This is the eternal contest; in this tangle time doesn't pass.

In our house there are strict rules for these contests. First they are conducted in the parents' bedroom where the carpet is soft. Second, I am required to sit Indian fashion in the middle of the floor away from the hard edges of furniture and open to attack from all sides. Third, as soon as any child starts crying, time-out is called and contenders are enlisted in an effort to nurse the wounded back to smiles.

The rules are intended as a civilizing force, there to soften blows, but the goal is ruthlessly Freudian: knock down Dad.

Last night in the midst of flailing arms and legs I was reminded of my teenage son when he was the age of my three-year-old. It was a different house, a different rug, a different scrawny body, but the contest was the same: the determined pee-wee charge, the lift and scream, the loopings of a child's doughy arms in the hairy arms of a father.

My older son no longer joins in the fray. We were wrestling as usual one night last year, all four of the kids this time, the three younger children a kind of warm-up team for the main act. Then the lanky thirteen-year-old stood before me, looking ready at last to settle old scores, and I knew I was doomed. He had youth, strength, and determination on his side of the room. All I had on mine was weight. Several hearty lunges was all it took. I came toppling down, the cheers of tiny voices ringing in my defeated ears. In the process, I accidentally jabbed him in the eye and took a stinging blow to the cheek myself.

He has not been back to wrestle since, leaving the contest to another generation of siblings. It is not just the victory, I suspect, that keeps him out of the battle now, nor for that matter his age. There is something else: a touch of mortality in the blows we exchanged, a sense that here at the edges of this innocent game lies a source of real danger.

His victory redefined a concept we both had quite comfortably assumed—the invincibility of the father. My loss in the game was a marker of my limits in his eyes. The sting on his cheek signaling as well the limits of my ability to protect him. When the dangers are real, the landings are not always soft, even when Dad's there. That was the subliminal lesson he took with him, I think, when he walked off rubbing his wound. That, I suspect, keeps him from coming back for more.

The younger generation has not given up though, and I, apparently, have no choice. They have taken to calling the game "Mongoose" for some reason and prowl about like the weasely snake killer. I, of course, am the snake.

The news is that last night my eleven-year-old daughter, with help from her little friends, delivered another bitter blow by toppling me again. The snake was out-weaseled. I blame this loss on gravity, in all senses of the word. In the face of so many attackers, and in the knowledge of ultimate defeat, it is hard to hold your head up. There is, one realizes, when his arms are pinned by tots and he is toppling with comic slowness under the weight of a screeching eleven-year-old girl, a sense of the absurdity of struggle, a feeling that forces larger than the self have taken over, infusing this meager game with grave significance. It is, I guess, from such small defeats that I am to salvage larger victories.

Once she had knocked me down, my older girl invited her younger comrades to sit with her on top of me. Like some elephant they had brought down in the jungle of family life I lay compliantly before them as each added a huffing weight to my load. Gravity. They had wrested a victory from me, from *Dad*, and were about to enjoy its sweets. Darker implications would sink in later. My daughter sat triumphantly on my back, arms crossed on her chest. The little kids screamed "mongoose! mongoose!" in a giddy chant. I lay underneath the pile, breathless, and laughing at us all.

Family is easy to write about because it is always around. It is, in fact, too much with us, many writers complain. Most of my friends who write prefer to wrestle their demons alone and have developed strategies for composition which amount to little more than escape from family. They are up before dawn or—at the other extreme—swill coffee and write past midnight. They build attic hideaways, as William Carlos Williams did, or cabins in the woods like Thoreau, who didn't even need a family to have the urge to escape one.

Writers never truly get away, though. Madeleine L'Engle has a writing cabin located in the woods behind her house, but, being partially blind, has a line running from house to cabin to help her find her way there—and back. We all have that line, though we string it in our minds and, when we disappear too far into solipsism, feel the tug viscerally. For a long time I, like other writers, tried to escape family, too, until one morning while looking at thirty canceled lines of poetry in *my* dusty hideaway I heard my daughters singing "It's All Right to Cry." I tossed the poem in the wastebasket and joined my children's voices. Suddenly I knew my subject.

We never get entirely away from families because they *are* us. They share our faces and voices and smiles and ground us in the familiar. Finding a crayon in the suit pocket or a jack in the shoe keeps us where we belong. Family gets our attention with shouts and mayhem—ask any father at the bottom of the heap in a wrestling match—and teaches with a curse, as it did on the day that I stepped barefoot on my son's toy moose. It speaks to us through all that remains unspoken in the sullenness of teenagers, the anxiety of sleepless nights, or the silence after a quarrel, and it instructs through weakness, its beauty resulting from the fragility—even goofiness—of its defenses against oblivion. My job, I came to see, was to write all this down.

Despite the fact that they are always there, families (like the children they spawn) don't stand still, and while I wrote about mine, it changed. I don't swim any more though in these essays I do. Nessa is not eleven, as she was when I wrote the first part of this introduction, and doesn't lower herself to wrestling with papa. Alice talks fine now—all but the vestige of her kid-talking lisp (the subject of one essay) gone from her speech—and Sam (the hero of that essay) has discarded his thumbsucking ways and reads with ease. Most of the essays were written between 1988 and 1991, years in which the family, animated by the fits and starts of its various members, slouched its way through many stages, but in several essays done nearly a decade ago we are so much younger that I hardly recognize those people any more even though they sing my songs and speak my sentences.

Wrestling with a family that never goes away and never stays the same has taught me that paradox is at the core of family life and is its two-beat, throbbing heart. Every mother is a daughter and any father a son. The father gives his daughter away as she becomes the apple of his eye, and a son grows into manhood by walking away from the father he resembles more each passing day. In family, such daily defeats are lifetime victories, but they never feel that way, the outcome of the war always in doubt and a matter of faith. We take on and shed roles with apparent ease among relatives, often unaware of all that such changes mean, but at each step stand humbled by the power of family to shape who we are. As Philip Roth has written, the son hauls the fetid bed pan of his aging father and agonizes over the symmetry.

These forms—revitalized by each new life that suffers them—
make up our most physical and concrete defense against oblivion,
the ecstatic cry and shiver in the lovers' dark, a meeting place for the
past and future. All of our celebrations—our many birthdays—come
to little more than an acknowledgment of this fragile, generative,
and familial *now* caught between two eternities. So we light candles
year after year and blow them out to the cheers of those who share
our blood, waiting in the dark for our piece of cake.

Young Harris, Georgia
Fall 1988–Summer 1991

The Nuclear Family

A witch cackles from my family tree. That is the word I got in the mail the other day when a family genealogy arrived. In addition to the good news that a progenitor fought beside William the Conqueror in 1066 and some other distant relative is a distant relative of Captain John Smith, comes this juicy bit from one of my American ancestors: "Rebecca Shelly, hanged herself on August 26, 1692, in prison, Cambridge, Massachusetts, where she was held on a charge of witchcraft."

The rest of the genealogy pales by comparison, with the possible exception of a Tory sympathizer whose remains were "burned on the common" in Worcester, Massachusetts, in 1790 and the headstone of his grave "put under the sod." Most of the genealogy is given over to a list of farmers, burghers, and professionals who braved life's common tragedies and wrote letters about prairie migration thick with—ho hum—everyday heartaches. But there *is* a witch and a hanging! It made our day.

In fact, the genealogy came just in time. Nessa needed it for a school assignment on her family history. Before she finished everyone in the house was caught up in the project—everyone except me. Matt drew the chart, the single slot which held Nessa's name swelling geometrically into a thicket of lines, branches on the family tree. Barbara searched boxes of old photos and spent time sitting at the kitchen table bouncing a pencil tip on her forehead and racking her brains for names. Nessa printed each entry carefully, marveling over the way maiden names cropped up later as middle names in our family and proud that her old-fashioned first name, Agnes, belonged to her grandmother and great-great-grandmother.

There were many smiles when the work was done, each name perched properly on a branch. Only I hung back, non-plussed. So many of the names were just that, names—no stories, no words, no memories, no faces. Holding the chart up, after the rest had gone to sleep, I saw that this family tree was all grid, a genealogy reduced to geometry. Who *are* these people? I wondered. Who *were* we?

Family photos have the same effect on me. Flattened out on the dining room table their glossy surfaces turn liquid and tempting under my fingertips but remain stubbornly opaque, oddly distant artifacts of familiar faces in strange places and strange faces among familiar ones. What do these silent, smiling people, drowned in the past and sealed within a photograph, have to do with me? A chin, a nose, a grin—I isolate these between my fingernails and patch together a semblance of faces I know, but, like scraps of today's torn picture blown and scattered into the past, these parts cannot be assembled into a coherent whole.

I think of those staged pictures made in tourist traps throughout the West: a painted backdrop of some frontier scene with holes in it for the faces. Poke your face through the hole and you are a cowboy or a cowgirl or—for an extra laugh—a cow. Are my family photos any less odd? The bits of me and the ones I love superimposed on unfamiliar backdrops?

And what about the faces I know well? They belong to people I love, true, but I took the photographs precisely because their images are not mine to keep. They are faces I visit—not the ones I live with—and there is always about their glossy expressions the look of someone surprised by a guest. I may call where they live home, but I am never at home when I'm there.

So where *is* home? My own biography, the severed ends of many genealogical lines, sputters and thrashes about the eastern half of the country trying to find its own place. Born in Dodge City, Kansas, I moved, age one, with my family to New York, was raised in Chicago, Kentucky, and New Jersey by two mothers, went to school in North Carolina and—after living briefly in three more states—settled in Georgia. I have attended colleges in North Carolina, New York, Maryland, Vermont, and Virginia, accumulating so many transcripts that the dread of paper work alone keeps me from applying for a new job. Since then, my wife and I have had four children born in three states. With a record like that it is pretty hard for the past, rumbling along at the leisurely pace of a Conestoga, to catch up.

Most of us have little choice in all this. A friend of mine, living out his version of the tale common to us all (an Indiana boy who married a Californian before settling down in Georgia) tells a story about his father. One morning before dawn, the father roused him out of bed and took him to the middle of a corn field. It was cold, the sky iridescent like mother of pearl. The boy was soon to go to college—never to live on this farm again. His father bent down in the stubble, grabbed a handful of black dirt, and put it in his son's hands.

"This is your mother," he said. "This is your father."

When he tells the story, my friend—who is now a biologist—bends over and makes a scooping motion, his hand inches from the carpet. He holds the fist out and cannot keep from smiling at the glory of the memory, and then shakes his head, opens his hand, the dust of his imaginings drifting through his fingers, blown away by the winds of reality. My friend is in red-clay country now, far from the good soil of his midwestern "mother" and "father." In our world, his father's injunction is little more than a wish, a longing.

There are stories in my family too—stories intended to connect me to a heritage—but they also sift through my fingers leaving me empty-handed. In June of 1870 my great-great-grandmother made the five-hundred-mile journey from Pella, Iowa, to Glen Elder, Kansas. Her memoir of the move, recorded by my grandmother in 1928, is rich with stories, humorous and moving by turns. *Item*—the heartbreak of packing: "I insisted on a dresser, a commode, and carpet for my bedroom and sitting room, but we finally cut it down to the commode and carpet with a full set of nice dishes. Then we filled every available place with loose oats for the horses." *Item*—the terror of locusts: "On August 1, 1874, there was an eclipse of the sun. Later, one of our men got up from the dinner table, went to the door and said, 'there must be another eclipse.' I looked up at the sun and said, 'it is the largest swarm of bees I ever saw.' In less than 10 minutes everything was covered with grasshoppers. At 2 o'clock we went to the cornfield, you could hear them chomping like pigs. They ate the covers, husks, cobs and leaves, leaving the bare stalk. They even ate the onions into the ground." *Item*—the joy of new birth: "My first child was born during the winter of 1870 with the assistance of a neighbor woman. That morning the snow sifted through the roof into my bed."

These are wonderful stories, my heritage, but they do not belong to me. I have moved so far from them—in place and spirit— that they are someone *else's* tale, no more real to me than the history of William the Conqueror.

I live, like most Americans, in a "nuclear family," a term best defined as "the contents of a mini-van or less." Grandparents keep out. For sociologists who coined the phrase a nuclear family is "an independent, autonomous unit" in which "each marriage marks the start of a new conjugal family, separate in residence, self-supporting, and in control of its affairs." In short, a nuclear family is one without a place or history.

The term seems apt, suggestive of the kinds of annihilation common to family life in America, especially these days. It is nuclear, in the literal sense, because it is a core family, shrinking away from the sustaining larger family of grandparents, uncles, aunts, and cousins. It is nuclear, too, because, under the pressure of modern life it is prone to split, with devastating effects to all involved. The phrase is a comment on the chances of survival, a reckoning of the odds. And, as the words suggest, the odds are terrible. Few families can take each other for the span of a generation these days without one partner packing up the mini-van and heading west.

The result: families become names in a book, genealogies compiled by experts that have no place in the heart, passion without an object for some, mere curiosity for most.

Something is missing in the nuclear family. I sense the absence most concretely, I think, when I am in the midst of a family fight and realize, in my fury, that there is no one outside this throbbing nucleus to turn to. Shouts, slammed doors, and angry thumpings reverberate in the house's shell and return uncushioned by the long faces of a larger family. No one hears what I say or cares; no one is there to rescue me from myself. When the fight is over, I look out my picture window and see my image fill with the darkness of the alien landscape that, by default, I call home.

What is remarkable here—as always—is the resilience of the human spirit, the resourcefulness of Americans cut off from a nurturing family culture. "There was no lumber this side of Junction City and very little there," my great-great-grandmother said. "So we built our house of rock with dirt roof, holes for windows and doors. To close these we used my carpet." She knew the meaning of nuclear family. Cut off from supplies in Pella, she "made do"—to use a phrase familiar to Kansans—and built her house into the ground.

We make do, too. Far from any home or history, the nuclear family invents traditions on the spot and by its own lights—nonce rituals, the free-verse of family life. Like suckers rising from the roots of felled family trees, these ersatz ceremonies have the beauty of a blossom mixed with pathos of a stump. They may not brighten the night, but they gladden the day, serving by their newness as a reminder of lost grandeur. Traditional rituals—the Moravian Feast of Lights, for instance—honor the past by codifying it. The cookies must be baked this way. The candles must be lit at this hour. Re-enactment, repetition is the point. Nonce rituals, on the other hand, make up for lost historical richness with spontaneity. Silliness is never codified out of nonce rituals nor are these on-the-spot rites battened down by martinets of tradition. Silliness is, in fact, the defining ingredient.

One of the best nonce rituals I know of was invented by a family who live near us, a nuclear family of the fundamentalist stripe, one that adds to its isolation by keeping the children out of public schools and enforcing strict codes of learning and behavior. In this family there is no TV or rock and roll. And yet the family, especially the children, never seems stiff or doctrinaire—quite the opposite, in fact, as though the isolation from conventional society allows for true idiosyncrasy. Each summer this family celebrates itself by an odd ritual: the father wakes the children in the middle of the night, takes the whole bunch to a park, and lets the children, armed with flashlights, play on the swingsets, slides, and climbing toys in the pitch dark. I imagine them playing into the early morning, the shadows of the swingset elongating into a tripod for the moon, the see-saw jutting a dark plank into a glitter of stars, and the bobbing heads of children casting flashlit shadows against the Milky Way. How different their giggles must sound at night—more like whinnies in the wind than laughter! The activity, so simple and yet so subversive of the quotidian, is a nonce ritual.

In our family, I announce the first snow by whistling "Dixie." No one knows how this started, exactly, although it, too, was invented to handle the problem of having children home from school. We live in the Georgia mountains, only a few miles from the border of North Carolina, and get a couple of bus-stopping snows each year. When that happens, I trudge off to work wrapped in a scarf and bundled to the chin, carrying my suitcase and looking respectably bound. The kids, snowed-in, are left behind for the day. I'm whistling, oh, say, some bit from Beethoven's Seventh. No sooner am I out of sight than the kids begin plotting, making piles of snowballs and settling down for the day in some hiding place behind a tree or a snow-drifted wheelbarrow, waiting for my return.

They know I'm coming when they hear me whistling "Dixie"— the signal that I've shed my briefcase and am ready for battle. Why "Dixie"? Why whistling? Who knows? But I certainly am not *just* whistling "Dixie": I'm a moving target. Suddenly there is a blur of white in the sky as my bundled body absorbs the first blows. I trudge forward—throwing a few hastily packed snowballs of my own—awaiting the next volley. Along the way I may upright a little kid who, turned over in a snowsuit, rocks in the drifts like a flipped turtle, my good deed rewarded by a direct hit to my rear! The rest of the time I trudge ahead, occasionally catching a snowball and tossing it back. The important thing is that I never miss a beat. Red cheeks puffed and lips stoically puckered, I keep on whistling.

Maybe I whistle "Dixie" because I'm a lost cause against children armed with snow and ice. At any rate, by the time I totter up the steps I look like Frosty, white from top to bottom, with a hint of rebel red in my cheeks. My wife greets me at the door with a stiff Jack Daniels.

The nonce ritual that fits our family best is Birthday Bird. Most of the year this puppet droops in tangles in a downstairs closet. But on our birthdays we hang it for a week from the lamp over the dining room table where it serves as a daffy reminder that someone is a year older. Matt brought it home as a shop project when he was in sixth grade. "The other class made guns," he complained. "We made these dumb ducks!" He held his duck up for all to see. It twisted under his fist, legs crossed, head drooped, and tail high in the air.

"I think it's *perfect*," his mother said, taking the toy from Matt and shaking a few kinks out. "I know *just* what to do with it." She hung it from the dining room lamp where it stayed until somebody had a birthday. From then on it was Birthday Bird.

Although Matt called it a duck, Birthday Bird is more properly classified as a generic bird. Each of its parts—tinker-toy feet, yarn legs, ovoid body and pointed head—is unrecognizable as anything birdlike by itself, but bobbing above the cake candles in graceless consort, the bits of string and wood do come to resemble *some* kind of bird. Proto-bird, perhaps. *Birth*day bird. Touch one piece and all parts dance and jiggle like a tickled baby. Let it stand for hours and breezes still play on it causing the body to twist with rotisserie slowness, the feet rising and falling, the head nodding. Often it seems to be watching you, the black eye swimming your way momentarily, but soon this apparent attention is shown for the sham it is as the eye—like a lawn sprinkler set on slow—keeps moving along its path, ruled not by sympathy but by the inner compulsion of its strings and parts, oblivious to all outside.

I think of the solar system, suspended mid-space, each part hanging free and moving in harmony. I think of snow swirling down on a baby's brow and a witch turning in the noose of her own sheets. I think of the atom, electrons whirling in a sub-visible blur around a miniscule nuclear core. Looking at Birthday Bird I think of all things tangled, goofy, doomed and suspended in space. For our family it is, as Barbara said, "perfect."

All rituals are about loss, the insubstantiality of life, but nonce rituals tug at us in other ways, too. They take on a fresh poignancy since they are as flimsy as the flesh they represent. The Feast of Lights will last as long as there are Moravians to celebrate it, long after Birthday Bird slumps in rotting strings and tumbles from the perch. Birthday Bird is a symbol of all that flops out of our grasp. Rather than commemorate life, as traditional rituals do, the ritual of Birthday Bird ratifies loss.

In this it is like words, pictures, and all other reminders of life's passing masked as mementos. I line up the kids for a picture in a kind of frenzy, sacrificing the tranquility of the present to an uncertain future, saving forever a moment lost to posing. Even then I suspect I'm in trouble. When the pictures come back from the drugstore I flip through them registering all that is missing, the absences and gaps in these visual memorials. Built out of the fear that all is insubstantial and tentative, they are no balm, but symptoms of the problem. They offer no solace.

Words are no better. "After you've written, you can no longer remember anything but the writing," Annie Dillard complains. "After I've written about any experience, my memories—those elusive, fragmentary patches of color and feeling—are gone; they've been replaced by the work. The work is a sort of changeling on the doorstep." Photos, words—they, like nonce rituals, shadow reality. A word to the wise is never enough, and a picture worth a thousand of them merely multiples the insufficiency. With Birthday Bird at hand, the bird in the bush gets away.

On the night of a recent birthday of mine, I stayed up alone and watched the old bird twist in its strings. There was no wind, but eyes and head floated slowly, propelled by some inner restlessness or some otherwise invisible agitation. Suspended in glittering nylon the painted eye caught mine. I glanced away; it kept spinning, oblivious to me as always. No comfort. Suddenly I saw how little of our lives we keep and was afraid. Like the mourner walking away from the grave, I was alone with loss. "This is *it*?" I asked, setting down my drink and casting a cold eye on the dumb bird. Against the inevitable losses of family life—of all life—I bring a marionette and whistle "Dixie" in the dark?

There is, after all, a sorcery in all this hocus-pocus of the everyday. Like a witch, I surround myself with owl, cat, and bat—beasts of nocturnal solidarity. Whistling "Dixie" is my incantation for another season and Birthday Bird is my eye-of-frog-and-tail-ofnewt concoction for another year. With this witchcraft I hope to untangle my life's strings and fly by night. I steal children, taking them far from any home, until one day—*presto!*—I too vanish into thin air. Looking at Birthday Bird I think of a black figure twisting undiscovered in a dark-lit cell. Maybe there really *is* a witch in my past.

A picture comes to mind: a mini-van hurtling down a black highway, illuminating a patch of road ahead and followed by the reddish dark it drags close behind. *This* is the nuclear family, and our pictures and rituals and words are never enough to redeem the losses. No witchcraft will keep the noose from drawing tight.

Nonce, noose, nuclear—our losses, it is true, are never redeemed. All that you love, you lose.

And yet I come back the next night as I do on any night the bird hangs from the ceiling light, to watch its silent spin yet again. Gazing into its mingle of threads and bobbers, midnight snack in hand, I feel happier, better, awash perhaps but still afloat and less alone. Our tawdry ceremonies—patch and paste for families with no past—draw us in quiet moments as if they had one more thing to whisper from the gloom. Draped from a pole here, hung on the wall there, or riding a breath into a cold night sky, these decorations of the present serve as reminders that the beauty of the modern family is not its success in the face of death but the quixotic nature of its resistance, the goofy defenses it has made against oblivion. They drape uncertain beginnings—weekends, seasons, birthdays—in the familiar and bear this message: the world may or may not outlive us and our children, but it will, in all probability, survive tomorrow, and most of us will have the humor necessary to cope.

For the nonce, that had better be enough.

Kid Talk

When Sam was a baby he slept with a bookmark. At bedtime he trotted off to his room, the prize fast in his fist, his blanket trailing behind. Before falling asleep, he held it under his nose, rubbing it between his thumb and forefinger. Conscientious parents, we tried to retrieve the marker—save the place in the book, we said— but the place was in Sam's heart, and he insisted that the slip of paper go with him. At night, when we checked on the kids, Sam's bookmark was invariably curled in the fingers he held to his lips, keeping for another night the place where words end and dreams begin.

I was in graduate school at the time, a parent enduring a return to school. The knowledge that Sam was asleep with his marker while I plowed through literature in my library carrel was a comfort. Surrounded by shelves of books, I felt Sam's spirit, and when I trudged home under campus lights, I was comforted by the thought that Sam was there doing his bit—somnolently.

Sam wanted to do what the rest of us in the family do: read books and talk about them. By marking his dreams he hoped to lay claim to the riches of his parents' language. But Sam was not there yet. Linguistically, he lived in the halfway house between the silence of the womb and the chatter of school. At the cusp of adult speak, he was inevitably betrayed by his own words which identified him as a bona fide, if reluctant, speaker of the only native tongue: kid talk.

Actually, Sam, who knew no verbal fear, had a genius for kid talk. Bestial and vegetative mutations came to metaphorical life on his tongue. His landscapes were darkened by "dinahorsies," his mother wore "bazebras," and his half-pint girl friend, a colleague in kid talk, wore "bukinis." When Sam got angry he told me that he would not only refrain from blowing me a kiss, he wouldn't blow me a hug either. "God is good, God is gray," his dinner prayer began, ending, appropriately, with a breathy "ah me."

In fact, Sam is one in a long line of verbal innovators in our clan. Matt, his older brother, came up with "piber bebs" for spider webs. He called spoons "boonas" and invented "vatermeloons" one summer day when I cut one open for a picnic. At age two—the *annus mirabilis* for most kid talkers—his sister, Nessa, called feathers "fedders" and talked about "ambliopsies" when they screamed by, lights flashing. The tradition continues with Alice, our current baby, who calls footprints "foot friends," and, bouncing from one family member to another, has invented the perfect transition for categorical ambiguity, "butcept." She spends her winter months brightening the yuletide with "Merry Fritzmas."

Born of baby babble and peekaboos in a mother's arms, kid talk is the language of pampering and cozy enclosures. Nurtured in this loving haven, it takes on the power of the incantation, the gnomic phrase, and is both magical and indestructible. Who knows how it happens? Something transpires in the clearing of the child's mind, where all is spooky and dripping and resonant. Mere words, dragged into the mushroom circle of the innocent imagination, are stripped of worldly trappings and—hearing a new music—made to dance. They are transformed, turned into kid talk which, upon utterance, casts an irresistible spell. Kid talk survives the condescension of Art Linkletter, the intellectualizing of Lewis Carroll and the studied gropings of a writer like me. Kid talk is where we start; inevitably, it takes us home.

Sometimes the way home is long. When Nessa was little and refused to walk home on her own steam, I used to con her with "Dinky," a poem by Theodore Roethke. I promised that if she would walk with me back to the house, I would recite "Dirty Dinky" for the distance. The poem was, without a doubt, born in the childhood clearing of Roethke's mind. It describes life at the meteorological extremes: deserts, snowy nights, and worm-wet storms.

"Oh what's the weather in a Beard?" it asks, and answers: "It's windy there and rather weird." It is in such weather that our calamities occur, the poem tells us, and each stanza ends by putting the blame squarely where it belongs—on Dirty Dinky.

The poem is spooky and funny and full of surprises. When you find yourself on a "hot, hot plain" or if you "step barefoot on a worm"—in short, no matter what gooey, nasty thing you do—Dirty Dinky takes the rap. "Dinky" ends with all the foreboding its silliness allows and so strikes, in the uncanny way of kid talk, somewhere close to the truth. Calamities, we learn, are the products of inner, not outer, weather. The storms of our lives are all in our heads. The culprit—the Dirty Dinky—is us. "*You*," the poem ends, "may be Dirty Dinky."

Roethke, forever a child in earnest, returned consciously and obsessively to the riddle-magic of children's language. Sylvia Plath, who learned from Roethke, produced some of her finest poems from kid talk as well. Her celebrated piece "Daddy" is best understood in this light. There is anger in this poem, but it is not in the mature voice of the woman launching an attack against patriarchal society. Rather, this is the anger of the spoiled child, the kind of voice that is usually accompanied by pouting, foot stamping, and crossed arms.

> You do not do, you do not do
> Any more, black shoe
> In which I have lived like a foot . . .
> Barely daring to breathe or Achoo.

Stamp, we hear in the background. The little girl pouts.

The poem is about the fury of being orphaned in the world. Kid Talk, language loved for all it cannot say and so the genre for absence and poignancy, is the perfect vehicle. These words mean what they sound and sound what they say. Plath spent most of her last years awaiting the "spasmodic . . . radiance" of a childhood heaven while fleeing the burdens of adulthood on earth. The kid talk of her craft—of poetry—took her where she longed to go.

Such non-utilitarian uses of language inevitably take on a phosphorescent glow and share a genre niche with other apparently useless or outmoded ways with words. Kid talk functions, for instance, like a riddle in which getting the point is withheld but not lost, and words take on all the beguiling mystery of what they have not yet said, promising more than they can deliver. At the same time, kid talk is the language of the oracle delivering on all it promises and more, telling us what we know deep in our hearts but won't admit. It drives us, as it drove Oedipus, back to the family we flee.

At one extreme, kid talk is the gooey mumbling of babies, the incomprehensible sucking and cooing at the mother's breast. It articulates contentment and suggests mystery. But kid talk tugs incorrigibly at the pantleg of adults, too. Freud lumps slips of the tongue with "symptomatic actions" from which, he argues, "one is justified in inferring" the presence of "restrained or repressed impulses." In short, the kid in us breaks out. Kid talk, then, is the embodiment of free, or better, *freed* expression for child or adult. In the cage of daily life it is, like hope, the thing with fedders.

And yet, the lovely language of children is not entirely innocent: the cozy world of family talk can suffocate. Who hasn't been subjected to the tedious argot of someone else's family life—the poopsie, sweetie-chums, huggums talk that should be outlawed for all but consenting adults and their offspring? Kid talk can cloister us in contented silliness and turn our conversations into a parade of jokes which, like home movies, amuse the family and bore everyone else.

In *Hunger of Memory* Richard Rodriguez writes seriously about the seductions of family talk by describing the way Spanish, the language of his parents, functioned in his childhood home in Sacramento, California. It became a protective envelope of sounds, detached from everyday meanings, the totemic language of lonely exiles, ripe for idiosyncratic variations and linguistic mutations, a lovely simpering:

> Some nights, no one seemed willing to loosen the hold sounds had on us. At dinner, we invented new words. (Ours sounded Spanish, but made sense only to us.) We pieced together new words by taking, say, an English verb and giving

it Spanish endings. My mother's instructions at bedtime would be lacquered with mock-urgent tones. Or a word like *sí* would become, in several notes, able to convey added measures of feeling. Tongues explored the edges of words, especially the fat vowels. And we happily sounded the military drum roll, the twirling roar of the Spanish *r*. Family language: my family's sounds.

The emphasis on sounds, the tendency to find emotional gold in verbal alchemy, the privately articulated "measures of feeling"—these are the characteristics of kid talk. For Rodriguez, Spanish became a seduction from the commerce of everyday life and a refuge from the realities of his adopted culture. The language of home kept him at home, away from the public arena which defines self: "What I needed to learn," Rodriguez wrote, "was that I had the right—and the obligation—to speak the public language of *los gringos*." The rest of the book chronicles Rodriguez's struggle to learn the language of public discourse and the pains and losses he suffered along the way.

In fact, all kid talk cloys after a time, whether it comes from poets, embarrassed adults, the writers of children's books, or kids. Who, except a child, does not sicken of Dr. Seuss's anapests, skipping as many as possible on the third or fourth or fiftieth bedside reading to an astoundingly resilient kid? If "Dinky" carries us through the morning, what about the afternoon and the long, long night when the children go to sleep? Don't we tire of riddles and coyness? Dorothy Parker put the matter succinctly. Writing under the name Constant Reader, she concluded her review of *Winnie the Pooh* with this memorable indictment: "the Konstant Weader fwowd up."

Fortunately for Sam, the bearer of the bookmark, kid talk is not an endless labyrinth of broken speech. It is, rather, the thread which leads the child *out* of babble. Unless arrested by genius, kid talk adulterates the gushing womb-silence of the child's mind, and is a mark of growing up and going public.

Last year Sam wrote a poem for school on the subject of spring. In a burst of teacher-pleasing conventionality, he called the poem "Spring." It goes like this:

> Spring
> A caterpillar hatched.
> The sun comes out.
> All the animals shout.
> It is Spring.

Why do we like this little poem? Despite the first line which is goofy and off-beat, the poem is not original in the way, say, the word "dinahorsies" is. It plods through a conventional subject, conventionally. And yet—butcept—it does have a charm. I think we like its sounds, the way they flirt with a traditional quatrain but do not succumb to it, the missing rhyme in the last line winning us. What we like in the poem is the way Sam plays with our expectations and *almost* fulfills them. He is, we sense, at the edge of having his kid talk forever corrupted.

" 'These wings are great,' she said"—that was the beginning of a story Nessa wrote in sixth grade. The story, about a girl flying around a shopping center like an angel, needs some work, but the opening is priceless. We like it less for its innocence, though, than for the charm of a fresh imagination beginning to learn control. It is original—it has a surprise—but we are also attracted to its artistry: so much of the rest of story is in the opening. It has designs on us and so goes beyond kid talk. Language like this lifts my daughter, by skill and calculation, out of the home and into the lives of others. Such wings are great, indeed.

These words surprise, like pure kid talk, but carry as well the moment of recognition, the realization that we, like our words, function in a world beyond the mushroom circle of our making. They indicate an agenda outside of the family. Falling short of the jabberwocky of the gods, they have human purposes which shape those who speak and hear them. Sam and Nessa don't discover themselves in the babble they invent but in the words and forms they inherit. There is a continuum here, the giddiness of kid talk leading inexorably to coherence and communication.

When Matt was first born I took to reading the dictionary—an odd consolation for my lost youth. Like my baby son, I came upon new words one at a time. I discovered the word *caveat*, I recall, and used it in and out of proper context for a day—the next day a new word and so on. No doubt I was hard to live with, but the magic of individual words mesmerized me. Bewitched by sounds and eerie etymologies, I took words one by one in my mouth and devoured them like a poet.

Since then I have learned that the magic of language, once we pass the kid-talk stage, is not in the words but in the syntax—the magic is in connection, in meaning. Now I am in love with sentences, some of my favorites having lost all but a trace of kid-talking eloquence. They are lowly and lovely at once. "A man is rich in proportion to the number of things which he can afford to let alone," Thoreau wrote. Sounding like a cross between a math problem and a lawyers' lunch, the sentence is short on poetic beauty. *Rich, number, proportion, things*—these are the words that do us in, right? Put together, they sentence us.

And yet, Thoreau turns the words against themselves, the otherwise horrid sentence redeemed by one well-chosen surprise: the word *afford*. "A man is rich in proportion to the number of things which he can *afford* to let alone." What a wonderful turn *afford*, that cardboard word, gives the remark and how deeply it embeds Thoreau's message in our own dulled minds. The magic does not come from the word, to be sure, but from the set up—the play of words which allows materialistic expectations to be raised and reversed. It works by making a surprising, but *meaningful*, connection with an audience, forming the kind of bond with the reader that kid talk by definition severs.

With the language that others invest in us, we purchase a self, one that even a skinflint like Thoreau could not afford to leave alone. We bank on it, incurring a debt each time we open our mouths. At home with words, we are mortgaged to the hilt, negotiating ambitious plans for redemption in another—and another's—life. At times we look with longing to the world on the other side of the book mark, but the ledger is thick and we know we cannot go back. It is not mere worlds that separate us from our innocence, but a more formidable amortizer of the soul: words. Following the call of the wild a few brave poets bridge the gap and tell the tale but rarely come back alive. The rest of us toe the line: language on our side, silence on the other.

Dinahorsies and bazebras roam the border between.

The Eternal Seventh Grade

Nib, nub, bud; node, knob, bulb; wen, weal; pout, pome; hump, hunch, bunch; not dent, dint, dip; not plat, plate, plain; not flush, not flat, but bowl, bulge, bob; bud, blow, bloom.

Shell.

Arc.

Nest.

Cheryl Stark's breast—my seventh-grade obsession.

How do I speak of such a thing? This moonlit pillow, this deep sea anemone of the mind, this bowl of milk tipped my way by memory?

Four rows separated us, but I could plainly see, backlit by windows, the gibbous beauty of the new breast hidden in the folds of her blouse. An interior music played, a high whine, like the buzzing of flies, punctuated by a low blood-throb that turned my ears perpetually red. My nostrils filled involuntarily with odors: warm hay, manure, sweet-scented lilacs. My tongue did not hang out, surely, but I did taste something at its tip: a smarmy offering of the glands.

When Cheryl raised her hand the shadowy breast spread against her ribs in a pretty pout. When she sat at ease with her arms beside her, her back straight like a child's and eyes attentively ahead, the sunlight revealed a perfect biscuit-sized nub gathered in her bra. Usually the pure gold of flesh had to be sought out amid irritating cloth, but sometimes, when she yawned or stretched, blouse flattened against breast, image met outline, and all came clear: shape and shadow were one.

In the hall or on the grounds, I arranged to walk beside her, catching—when she bunched the books against her front—a glimpse of flesh in all that white of blouse and lace and straps. What I remember most, though, were not these stolen glances, but the hours of unobstructed, mesmerized gazing, seemingly endless hours of watching and watching and watching a shadow. Outside, the weather changed—baked-hot sun, ice-cold sun, gusty, tree-ruffling sun—but inside, conditions remained constant, a sun-struck pink shadow against the heaped-snow blouse, the image of awakening desire.

Life is flesh—that is the lesson of the eternal seventh grade. The lesson is not simply sexual, though the desks of this classroom are bolted to the body and lit by libidinous neon; it is, rather, an awakening to sensual delights born of the sexual impulse. The subject is not skin, but the play of light on skin, the flesh made word, and so has in it something of the divine.

Stalking the halls of elementary school for the sensually precocious and claiming sexual slow-learners on into high school, the eternal seventh grade hits people at different times. For many, though, seventh grade is the year. Monkish souls avoid it and certain libertines smash through the stage barely affected, but all of us find our name in the rollbook in the end. Once felt, the emotions are eternal, and eternally triggered by reminders of their first context. Any young breast will do. We see the little bulge and suddenly find ourselves, truants in a world of adult responsibilities, smiling wistfully in the detention hall of a happy thought.

Memory, in part, is the culprit, lending inordinate space to the seventh grade. A freckled-faced smile from that year begins in January and ends as a lipstick pout sometime in April. A wink lasts all spring and a dress hem requires a summer of solemn floating to cross a knee. A waist tapers from Memorial Day to Thanksgiving and plunges with a sizzling twist into the snows of Christmas—and every Christmas snow thereafter. In the seventh grade, eternity can be snatched from any hour and played back in a lifetime of sensual remembrances.

Prepubescent kids, the sixth graders of the world, are sensual, too, but there is a difference: once the babies leave the breast and throw off the blanket, they don't connect the sensual and the sexual in a conscious way. They can look at anything with the vacant gaze of the caressing eye. A stone, a leaf, a door—any object can take on the glow for these promiscuous, pre-teen lovers of all. When I was small, I liked to turn my bicycle upside down and pass the summer spinning my wheels. For hours I watched, mesmerized and lost. Time went on forever. In seventh grade I lost this capacity for disinterested observation, unless the object of my gaze was Cheryl's breast.

This narrowing of attention to the beauty of all that rises to the touch, hardens, and dies marks the eternal seventh grade. It is a wordless contemplation of concupiscence, a taking in, at the gut, of all that passion means.

A friend of mine who is a lesbian once described to me the first thing she noticed about her lover. It was her ear. She was drawn to the way it curled into itself like an orchid, the skin so thin light passed through it. "See," she said, touching her lover's ear, the fingertips lingering over a lobe that had been the glowing object of her long, long gaze, and I knew then that this feeling is universal. She, too, had dreamed her way into the front rows of the eternal seventh grade.

Seventh grade continues in adulterated form long after the school year is done. All through high school, the images of seventh grade drove me into darkened corners where I conducted experiments in newly learned rules of love with a girl named Bellamy Bourbon. God knows what Bellamy looked like—a pretty little girl, probably—but to my eyes she was the paragon of beauty. When I recently heard a friend recite the familiar Leigh Hunt poem about an English girl that ends with this plaintive, but ultimately comforting, line, "Say I'm growing old, but add, Jenny kissed me," I thought of Bellamy, who had, if nothing else, the most beautiful name in the world. It would suffice, I thought in high school, to touch the breast of Bellamy Bourbon and die. There are, no doubt, better impulses for living, but touching the source of our urge to love is good enough.

The quest for more is endless. In a sense we all fail seventh grade, eager recidivists rubbing the nub of our dream, repeating for the rest of our lives what we never master, all of our attempts compelled by an image burned into the retina of the mind's eye.

The comic conclusion of the year-long gaze of seventh grade is "making out," a subject beneath contempt for all but its leaden, breathless practitioners. What we are able to "make out" in this time of obliterated discernment is anyone's guess. My generation sunk into the plush seats of movie houses and groped for each other under the comforting glow of our illusions. There we encountered the problem of human symmetry head on, learning the clumsy way that nose must make way for nose if lips are to meet. What was a feast to the eye in the eternal seventh grade is flesh in the hand in the back rows of confirmed adolescence, a sensual gluttony accompanied by lip smacking, uncontrollable gaspings for air, a satisfaction felt deep in the viscera, and—well—leftovers.

The dark theater is a reminder that all is not light in the seventh grade. There is a smudgy residue to the otherwise lambent joys of sensual awareness, a hickey on the neck of seventh graders of all ages. In the throes of sexual awakening, something else happens. We look and look and look and then, lulled by the inward buzzing of our gaze, we catch ourselves looking and the game is up. The nub rubs raw.

I was in my older sister's room when self-consciousness struck, sitting at the edge of a bed strewn with teen magazines, still clinging to the battered edge of the perishable sixth grade. "Don't you just *love* him," my sister gushed to a friend on the phone. They were talking about a teen idol whose face was on half of the glossy covers. "Don't you love his *hair!*"

"The part's messed up," I complained, when she got off the phone. I held up one cover to prove my point.

"I *know*," she said grabbing the magazine out of my hand and dancing around the room with it pressed to her nightshirt. "Don't you just *love* it!"

Maybe *that* was opening day of the eternal seventh garde for me, my sister's offhand comment initiating a year of study in front of the bathroom mirror as I carefully parted my hair and then, with equal care, mussed it up again. For hours I was lost in the iridescent emptiness on the other side of the glass. Unfortunately, there is more to this painstakingly constructed image than at first meets the seventh grader's reflected eye, something grim, the equivalent in life of a vice-principal patrolling the dark corners of junior-high hallways: the knowledge of death.

I don't need to recall when it happened to me: the moment hangs like a fixture in my mind. One night—after a day of blind gazing—I got into my pajamas, crawled into bed, looked into the darkness overhead, and realized at last what I had often heard but had not comprehended: some day this *me* would be gone. We did not attend church, so there was no heaven to confuse the issue. One day *this* me, capable of thinking *this* thought at *this* moment, would be gone. Not gone somewhere, but *gone*. It would no longer *be*.

No sleep *that* night.

I threw the covers off, got up and flipped on all the lights in the room. That's better, I thought, but then I caught a glimpse of myself in the bureau mirror and felt again the visceral fires.

Gone.

I blazed a trail of houselights to my brother's room and woke him up. He was eight or nine. When I shook his shoulder, his eyes, to my great relief, popped right open, and even before he sat up he said what he said every day that year: "Do you wanna play knights?"

My brother had a set of brightly painted metal knights, and he spent most of his waking hours trying to talk the rest of us into playing games with them. As a bonafide seventh grader I had put away childish things, but that night toys seemed preferable to staring into death's mirror. He got down the box and we spread the knights on the floor: Lancelot in silver, Arthur in gold, Guinevere in a white robe, and—my brother's favorite—the Black Knight, with a red-tipped lance. I had the good guys, the silver and the gold, and my brother took the Black Knight, with Guinevere thrown in as a consolation prize.

We got down on the floor and played, our eyes only inches off of the rug. From this perspective the characters became animated with the spirit of my sleeplessness. All of the ingredients of the eternal seventh grade were in place—white, red, and black. From this dustball view of things, I saw my own eye in the circle of my brother's, looking back, while he toppled my love-struck surrogates with the bloodied tip of his innocent lance. Fresh from my nightmare I felt a truth I did not understand: Guinevere is always accompanied by her escort, the Black Knight with the blood-tipped weapon. The best in gold and silver succumb. And I saw, as my knights lay bleeding in my brother's dust, that Guinevere is worth the risk.

Unfortunately my brother fell asleep on the floor after his victory, sucking his thumb and clutching the Black Knight to his neck.

Gone, I thought, the horror flooding back.

Then I did something odd. I walked down the hall to the bathroom and flipped on the light, the colorless glare of neon giving a strange comfort. I looked in the mirror and started combing my hair, getting the part just right and then, mussing it up.

Death-fear is often born in the silences of the eternal seventh grade—a time when adolescents gaze wordlessly into the marrow of life and are reluctant to talk about anything, not to mention anything difficult. The reason adults are silent, of course, is simple: what is there to say?

My daughter, an actual seventh grader, came home from school one day and proclaimed that she was going steady. She showed me the ring, holding her hand out at the end of a cocked wrist and smiling coyly. Embarrassed, she covered her face with her hand and laughed, peeking at me between spread fingers. The next day she returned the ring, but for a while she was head of her class in the eternal seventh grade. Her romance was innocent enough, I suppose, but there was a boy, a schoolroom, and a row of desks. Light streamed in through the windows of dull classes. "What long gaze preceded this short romance?" I wondered. What shadows are to be found in the folds of this thought?

The other night my daughter came downstairs about 2:00 A.M. She couldn't sleep. I asked her why, setting my book beside me on the makeshift bedding I had spread out on the sofa. When she stepped into the circle of my lamplight I could see that she had been crying. "I don't know!" she shrieked, her eyes swollen, the pupils wide from gazing long into the dark. "I just can't sleep!"

What could I say?

Fortunately, our silence on the subject of death may be appropriate, even necessary. It may be the only way to learn that there is life beyond seventh grade, an eighth grade of the soul where the nub of each day is not rubbed raw but taken for granted, where every breath is not counted, and death finds an obscure corner on the shelf of other vital, all-consuming metaphysical issues ignored by adults. In the endless eighth grade *love!* makes room for love. Bodies are given, not lost, and souls in the bargain found. The endless eighth grade, there by default in all lives, brings with it the wisdom of spent passions. It may not have the intensity to last forever, but it does go on and on.

No matter how long we glide serenely in such eighth-grade grace, though, our lives are occasionally shot through with a flesh-bound intensity born of the long, long gaze of seventh grade, pierced by the red-tipped lance of our mortality. I still can't speak to the issue of our deaths, but I can talk around it. It has something to do with a breast hidden in cloth and the knowledge that one day I would reach, delirious, through shadows to touch it, all that the eyes had promised delivered in gloom to my fingertips: nib, nub, bud; bulb, blow, bloom.

Endless Imitation

My daughter Nessa sashays through the house in a long white robe that nightly falls from my wife's shoulders. To keep the hem from dragging the floor, Nessa stands tall and hitches the terry cloth up under her belt. The sleeves fall over her hands, but she takes up the slack by holding her arms out wide and high like a ballerina. Affecting a prissy look, she tours the downstairs, a celebrity throwing kisses to her one adoring fan, me. Eventually she returns to the clutter of her room with all the elegance of Columbia amid scattered toys of the New World.

Clothes, I'm reminded, make the child.

Our children regularly ransack a brightly painted army locker stuffed with dress-up outfits. The remnants of many Halloweens burst over the edges when they undo the latch. Orange plumes rise from the heap and tumble to the floor. Feathers, flounces, and furbelows float through clammy fingers; beads, bells, and boas leap to greedy hands. Swords and armor, brocaded dresses and flimsy chiffon things, Dracula's cape and Robin Hood's vest—these and various unidentifiable sequined suits magically appear to children who open the Pandora's box and try it all on. Fancy hats are saved for last, the straw bonnet, witch's cone, or plastic centurion helmet lending panache to any motley outfit.

In our house, dress up is the rule. It is not uncommon to sit down to Saturday breakfast with a bare-chested, pint-sized barbarian wearing a wide-brimmed pointed hat, a bandana, three necklaces, a sequined belt, and a plastic sword shoved down his pantleg. "Pass the sugar, *please*," you say in such company.

The costumes come, of course, with characters. Afternoons Nessa rounds up her gauzy and besequined little brother and sister for a game of Michelle and Lavinia. The kids are Baby Alice and Baby Sam who brave a terrifying world along with a gang of abandoned, imaginary waifs, Michelle, Lavinia, and Baby Perry, to name a few. Nessa is the school teacher, the mother, or the ever-vigilant elder sister saving her troupe from villains and the ravages of nature. Some days our bed—the site of many adventures—is a ship at sea carrying these charmed souls away from dangerous and exotic lands to safety in England or France. Other days it's a prairie schooner rumbling through hostile territory, tomahawks whizzing overhead. All the while Nessa, the ubiquitous nanny, scares the wits out of her tiny charges with wild-eyed screams about squid! and winds! and flaming arrows!

In Nessa's mind anything can happen. " 'Tend like we're in the middle of the ocean and sharks are everywhere," she says in her make-believe singsong. Invented skies darken the Karistan sea as some fresh calamity strikes from the gloom. Fins rise out of the carpet. A snout appears. All is not well for our trembling band. Suddenly a slimy, disembodied hand—conjured up by words—flops over the gunwale! Alice screams, Sam runs into the bathroom crying, and all hell breaks loose until I, walking blithely across water, bring the ship crashing into calmer seas by telling them to hold down down the racket.

At night, when the children go to bed, I come across the plastic and lace of who they were strewn everywhere, evidence that we shed many outfits on the way to becoming ourselves. One trip through the downstairs and my arms are full.

"Heaven lies about us in our infancy," Wordsworth wrote, a heaven and an infancy that have nothing to do with the games my children play. For him, heaven consists of the child's capacity for wonder, a pristine state easily damaged by conformity to adult ways. The apparently innocent make-believe of children bothered him a good deal. Games like Michelle and Lavinia "fit" the child's tongue to the ways and words of adults, the "dialogues of business, love, or strife." The "little Actor" too easily "cons another part" and loses a soul in the bargain, as if, the poet adds, her "whole vocation" amounted to little more than "endless imitation." Then "Shades of the prison-house begin to close."

When Nessa was little she used to play school in classrooms of the building where I teach. Many afternoons she lined up the desks, chalked a lesson on the blackboard, stood imperiously before the empty seats with ruler in hand, and let her kids have it. Ruthless in her pursuit of the ABC's for her imaginary pupils she would plead, cajole, and hector the group until lessons were mastered and the phantom class could be dismissed with a beatific smile. Day after day she "fit" her "tongue"—Wordsworth's phrase is perfect—to the language of her teachers as if her sole business in life were, alas, imitation.

Wordsworth has it wrong, though, if he thinks this is a corruption of the child. Nessa's need to pretend comes from some place deep in her. Protective rather than insidious, her imaginary friends emerge when the world presses in on her. At one time she had a menagerie of them with names like Buke, Tsi-tsi, Rivers, Jongi. Later the little ghosts split into two groups who battled in her imagination. Now there was a Bad Buke and a Good Buke, a Bad Tsi-tsi and a Good Tsi-tsi—a division and matching that allowed Nessa to do vicarious battle with the world by interposing two rows of phantom pygmies. The little barbarian draws a sword on us all, sure, but such imaginary protections seem entirely natural, as much products of the inner as the outer world.

Nessa gave her skills as an actress a test when she was nine by trying out for a part in a local production of *Annie*. This was her first try at acting beyond the family, and she was a little young for the lead. "I hope she gets the part of Molly," I told my Dad who was up from Florida visiting at the time.

During the auditions the girls read a scene in which Annie meets a policeman. The performances were all cute, but Nessa's had something else, a winning animation and calculated sincerity. When the cop shouted, "Hey you, little girl, come here!" her answer— "Who *me* officer?"—was coy and naughty. She's a natural, I thought, forgetting the hours she had logged in as pretender, forgetting that acting—the self in disguise—is the business of life. I felt a pang. My little girl who single-handedly fought back alligators from our bed and kept a classroom full of invisible school children in line, was being coached by a director on the subtleties of sounding like an orphan. Suddenly I didn't know her.

"She's got the part," Dad said after watching all the auditions.

"Molly?"

"No," he whispered. "Annie—and you're next."

He was right. The director called the young actors back and announced that Nessa had the lead.

A week later Dad was safely himself in Florida, and I had four bit parts: a butler, a politician, a man on the street, and, of course, the policeman. For the rest of the summer I didn't know who I was without checking my costume.

Nessa wasted little time mastering her part, slipping into the role of Annie at will. Within days she had whipped her sibling waifs into a gang of orphans. Gone were the Conestogas, the ships on carpeted seas, the prairie school in tornado country. Now Alice and Sam were Big Apple orphans draped, to be sure, in boas and armed with plastic swords but stumbling through a newly learned orphan dance routine while Nessa belted out "Maybe." For the little kids it was a game still, Alice in particular willing to fall out of character, literally at the drop of a hat. "You can't just walk *off*," Nessa would groan, hat in hand.

For her, acting was a game and more. Practice was play *and* a way of life. Not long after she got the part I found her in front of a mirror flipping her hand and tilting her head in a coy gesture of dismissal—the patroness discharging a servant for the weekend. She held the final pose a moment—it was perfect—then fell out of character, straightening her dress, and did the gesture over again. And again. And again. Later she used the movement in one of the servant dance numbers in *Annie*. Acting I realized, had never been just a game for Nessa.

In the car on the way to rehearsals she did vocal exercises—nah-ni nah-ni nah-ni nah-ni noh—finding the pitches she would need to get through someone else's day on stage. In the lobby between sets she went through her steps with a choreographer until she got the spirit as well as the movements right. On stage, she beamed long before the lighting crew did its work. For a summer she relinquished herself to an animation that originated somewhere so deep within her it was not ours or hers. My little girl was an orphan who belonged to everyone else.

Who am I, I often asked myself that summer as I slipped out of the pants of a cop and into the rags of a bum and out of the rags of a bum into the suit of Cordell Hull. Who is *she*, I also asked, this girl who runs across the stage and flings herself into the arms of a surrogate daddy named Warbucks while her real daddy in disguise watches from the wings.

In the evenings, after practice was over, we would stop for root beer at a convenience store and try to sort out our real selves from the pretenders. Here *I* was Daddy Warbucks, calling the shots and paying the bills, unable to hide a smile when the clerk behind the counter said that my daughter and I were certainly cut from the same cloth. Unfortunately, these nightly excursions into reality were mere pit stops on Nessa's journey. She was, that summer, on her way to becoming someone else, and there was no stopping her. Her transformation was made complete when she dyed her hair red.

Nessa is a blonde like me and at the time still had streaks of platinum baby hair mixed with the darker colors of adolescence. Under the lights her hair gleamed like poured water. Annie, though, is a notorious red-head. The director suggested a wig—a bright, curly, orangy-red thing that looked just like Annie from the comics. Nessa tried it through a few rehearsals but found that it got in the way when she sang and danced. Easily knocked awry, it often left her looking more like a lush than a little girl. Finally, we broke down and made a trip to the drug store. After three tries, the dye took and Nessa's platinum curls rusted to a deep red. Now when I tipped my hat to her—as a cop on stage or a Daddy in the root beer shop— there was no mistaking us for the strangers we had become. I had fathered an orphan.

Our lives took on the colors of our roles that summer, and the songs usurped every waking thought, the music of *Annie* brainwashing the entire family. No idle, silent moment was safe, susceptible as it was to yet another inane bar from one of the show's tunes. The songs were everywhere. "Maybe far away or maybe real nearby"—it didn't matter. We heard them, the lives we led and the lives we played intertwining, the script, life's harmony line, insinuating itself into our improvised days.

During the production of *Annie*, Barbara—Nessa's real mother—in an effort to keep some sanity in the house, did her best to drive a wedge between life and its imposter. She put a moratorium on all songs from the play. Waking to "a day that's gray and lonely" and falling asleep to the bittersweet assurance that "the sun'll come out tomorrow" for a dozen tomorrows, got to be too much. Barbara's attempts to keep the world of make believe out of the lives we were in earnest making did little good. The play took over the family in a way that was frightening.

The effect remains, despite the broken *Annie* tape and the discarded *Annie* poster. This year Nessa belatedly turned the age of the little orphan, and every time she says how old she is—"*eleven*"— with the coy and haughty tone I first heard at the play audition two years before, I'm flooded with memories of *Annie*. The script takes a toll on real life.

It was inevitable, I guess, that real life would take its toll on the script, as well. Halfway through the production of *Annie*, Nessa got sick. Opening night had been a hit, Nessa crooning her way into the hearts of the crowd. Performances improved as the week went on, and those of us in the chorus had begun to loosen up to the point that we could shuffle through a dance routine without counting in our heads or watching our feet. There was talk about extending the number of shows and earning enough money for a badly needed cyclorama. The Peacock Summer Playhouse, some said, might go into the black!

Then came a three-day break in the schedule, a party with neighbor girls in a tent, a late, late night, and, the upshot, Nessa was sick. She went through several shows with a fever and a sore throat. During her brief moments backstage she slept on a cot, and the forced smile of the orphan relaxed into my daughter's frown. By Friday night, with three shows left she stopped smiling altogether, even on stage.

On Saturday Barbara and I called a halt to illusions and decided that Nessa could not do the show. This orphan, we knew, belonged to us. Her fever, climbing over several days, had reached a very real 103, and every swallow was a gulp. Dressed in her costume, the trouper was ready to go, but I, cop and father, sent her to bed and called the director.

What struck me as important was the pressure that the part in a play had put on real life. The show must go on!—we felt the imperative in those words, though they were never said. It was not the disappointment of the other actors, the theater group, or the audience, though they were part of the sadness we felt when I carried Nessa to bed that night. Rather it was the expectation of joy that playing the part would bring, the sense of something lost in the chaos of our lives by not being up to a script composed by real-life interlopers. The con game had turned very serious indeed.

We had done the right thing. By the next day the fever was gone and, with some scratchiness in her voice, Nessa was able to do the part, smiling again, for a last show. Barbara stayed backstage to be with her between scenes, holding her mainly and kissing her a lot, a dose of real life to get her through life according to the script. Every so often the butler, the cop, the man on the street, and Cordell Hull came by to give her a kiss, as well.

Fortunately every acting role is temporary, the costumes shed, make-up wiped off, glasses, book, pipe, and other props folded up, closed, or put away. We shove the dress-up clothes back in the army locker, flattening the witches' caps and crumpling the knight's plume to lower and latch the lid, a wispy fluff of color often left poking out at one side an invitation to another day's adventure. Eventually even Annie runs out of tomorrows and becomes a real kid again.

It is, I suspect, this ephemeral nature of drama that causes the theater to be a superstitious place—filled with magic, mysteries, and taboos. What else is there to cling to? The tradition among amateurs of striking a set right after the last performance is an example. The last time that the crew is together and enthusiasm high, the job of striking the set meets a practical need and does more: it is an acknowledgment that lines learned by heart must be exorcised and, in the process, hearts broken. The more it hurts, the more it is needed.

The stage manager reverses drills and one by one the screws that pin illusion are buzzed out. Cardboard rooms collapse, canvas cities sag, and gaily colored flats are stacked indiscriminately and hauled away. Snatches of song rise out of the pandemonium, painfully mastered harmonies sung at last with ease and abandon, a tough bit of syncopation here and a troublesome dance step there, labored over for weeks—these bits are delivered flawlessly to the first and best audience, the actors and crew themselves, while the director shouts "c'mon, c'mon, we don't have all night!"

Striking the set enacts a ritualistic death—a communal clubbing—that all in an amateur show feel and need.

Make believe is unmade.

The sets of family life come down with less fanfare and more pain. Shed slowly, these roles bear the lumpy burden of reality, leaving us to ourselves only when we have come to see, too late, that they are as close as we ever get to being who we are.

I'm thinking of Nessa strolling through the house in her mother's robe. "*Fah*-ther," she intones, wafted my way on the breezes of her imagination. I expect my little pixie to be a damsel in distress, a beleaguered schoolmarm on the prairie, or the Statue of Liberty guiding souls into the New World. I'm in for a surprise. Holding the gown out by her fingertips she turns slowly like a model and curtsies.

"See my wedding dress?"

Wedding dress? I look at her with new eyes. Wedding dress!

I do see it—that's the scary part. The bridal veil, hooked to a band of pale spring flowers, falls like air behind her blonde curls. Satin ribbons of my imagining flutter around her arms, a visible breeze. Terry cloth pours to the floor heavy and thick and wound on itself as wedding gowns will do. A burial suit lasts forever, but the wedding dress—hints of flesh in all its gauzy stuff—is made to come off, a colorless, insubstantial husk to be stepped out of and, like the father, tossed aside. My little actress cons another part, indeed. For a moment Nessa, in her mother's robe, is a bride—and the thought of it scares me to death. My eleven-year-old stands before me, an epiphany of a hard truth in my daily masquerade.

It will be a long night.

"Our birth is but a sleep and a forgetting," writes Wordsworth, but what, then, about our sleep? Nights when I can't sleep I drop in on the kids and watch them. They sleep so easily, snoring lightly while "trailing clouds of glory" into the new morning. In slumber, they discard their masks becoming, by night, the sweet nothings they cannot be by day. They look so haphazard lying there in the twists of sheets like bodies tossed from the sky and falling where they may. Maybe in sleep we become ourselves—who knows?

Matt, my older son, is abstracted in sleep, like someone drugged. He simply isn't there. Alice lies spread-eagled, in complete trust and surrender, wearing the expectant look of a Keatsian maiden awaiting her first kiss. Sam, the barbarian, lies tamed at last, clutching his plastic saber and sucking his thumb, his last role still clinging even in sleep to whatever is left of him.

Unlike our other kids, Nessa is a light sleeper, never still, always animated by some borrowed force like a feverish child. Once when I came by at night to check on her she was sitting bolt upright in bed, talking to vague presences in the shadows of the room. "Fire!" she said, moving her fingers before her eyes, a child tormented among her newborn blisses. "Arrows," she cried, suffering the stings of endless imitation and looking right at me, "so many arrows!"

"It's okay, Nessa," I said, helping her back under the covers. "It's just me."

I said it as if there is such a thing, a "just me" and a "just her," as if there were someone other than an anonymous bandit under every mask. I, a butler father moonlighting as a teacher, said it to my orphan daughter beset by war-painted attackers on every side, but I doubt that it is ever true. There are simply too many of us to choose from.

The show-stopper in *Annie* was a number called "I Think I'm Gonna Like It Here." In it Annie is brought for the first time to the mansion of Daddy Warbucks. She walks across the set wide-eyed and dazzled, meeting the entire Warbucks entourage in the process. Acting, dancing and singing are called for in this scene, and the capper requires acrobatics. Servants stand on platforms that rise from the stage and pass Annie in their arms, the top two men hoisting her on their shoulders to make the peak, forming a white-shirt, black-tie pyramid with a splash of red at the top.

I remember the awkwardness of the adults the first time the choreographer took us through the number. Tripping up on the fancy footwork, we laughed at our incompetence. The director frowned. I also remember Nessa gliding over our arms, giggling all the way up as she sang her part. When she got to the top she threw back her head, spread her arms wide, and hit the high note, singing, it seemed, to the whole world.

"A natural," the director said.

I was one of the actors who hoisted Nessa for the final note, taking great pride each of the nights in my daughter. "Beaming," many said afterwards; Matt says "flaming" was more like it. Nessa, I told all who would listen, was mine: note of my note and mask of my mask.

By the last production, though, I came to see how little of my girl I get to keep, she rising not on my arms, but on the arms of some butler, some factotum, and drifting inexorably into the hearts of an audience of strangers. What is a natural actor except another definition of what it means to be human? What is "endless imitation" except a name for the emerging self? What is this human pyramid with a little girl rising to the top, out of the hands of her father into darkened rings of broken hearts beyond the lights, but a picture of growing up in a family?

All of us live out the life of Annie, the archetypal orphan, auditioning for a lead in the next script we can live with, yearning for the parents of our true selves, fighting back imposters—the Miss Hannigans eager to sell us out—and settling, in giddy dread, for Daddy Warbucks. For twelve nights Nessa played the orphan, a part she found in a costume box in our basement. In her mother's robe she finds the woman she will be. In any event, I'm upstaged. Nessa rises on the shoulders of others, eyes glittering in the lights, sings "I Think I'm Gonna Like It Here" for all she is worth, and flops out of sight, an orphan in all but name, landing in the arms of a stranger called Daddy.

Unheard Melodies

Metal doors slam shut, snuff out the wayward harmonies of the congregation, and release baby Sam and me to grass and sky. He arches his back, shakes little fists, and screams. I carry him quickly down a gravel path, leaving the pre-fab, cream-colored church behind, and make my way across a heat-shimmering parking lot to— of all things—a small, log cabin that serves as the rectory. I clatter through gravel in my good shoes and step clumsily over creosoted logs at the lawn's edge. Even before I reach the steps, I'm singing.

The porch is austere: plain, rough-hewn, unpainted boards without a railing. It is swept clean, a metal shoe scraper and a ladder-back chair the only adornments—one of those places where any noise seems an affront. In the grass, off to one side, a concrete statue of the Virgin tilts in the sun, taking in the heat and dust of the parking lot beatifically. "What does *she* know about *this*?" I wonder resentfully, leaning back. I lift Sam to my shoulder, squint from his screams, and keep singing—desperately.

The song begins as a hum, the notes tentative, barely audible above Sam's crying, and apparently random, but they do search out a tune, trying one pattern, rejecting it, and then trying another. It's a kind of thinking—mesmerizing and soothing—and after five minutes, the baby calms down with a shudder and a sigh, his caterwaul tamed to a few chirps. "Hush a bye," I hum, thinking of the words. A wasp rises to the railing and hovers, amused. Butterflies flash their skirts. "Go to sleepy little baby." Sam yawns and smacks his lips contentedly. Even the Virgin, tilting forward still, seems interested.

Why sing? Songs soothe the baby of course, but why this song delivered without much prompting from the unconscious mind? And why, after Sam finds his thumb and calms down, do I keep right on singing, more for myself than for him, caught up by it all? This is not the kind of transporting narcissism that comes over me when I deliver opera full voice from behind the shower curtain, my bad notes lost in the reverberations, nor is it the mild conceitedness that tugs at me when, after a few beers, I clear my throat, strum a chord on the guitar, and try to sound good. It is a matter for my ears only (if I discount the ears of a concrete statue and an uncomprehending child), too private and subdued to be considered a celebration. Nothing is communicated and no emotions are purged or affirmed. (That is going on next door.) This mumbling is more like prayer, the introspective, tantalizing singing that we "incline an ear to"—the way Mary, accustomed to this kind of petition, is doing.

In fact it seems as if I'm not singing a tune at all but thinking or mulling it over. An inner argument, delivered by a thread of sound, holds me—not the sound itself. I teeter on the back legs of the chair and take in the heat-shimmering landscape: the cluster of bedraggled shrubs, the glittering gravel parking lot, the hoods and tops of cars throwing off plates of light, and, beyond all that, the wide, deep hayfield stretching out to a dark stand of cedars. Like prayer, the song makes the world around me seem ephemeral and a bit unreal.

Something is trying to break through.

Songs remember—that's why we sing them to ourselves. They help us to recover what we were. I'm twelve or thirteen, hunched in front of a record player—a "Silvertone," the portable type with detachable stereo speakers. The turntable rests on the floor near my bedroom window. The door is shut, the room's curtains drawn down. The reflection of my face spins on the platter, but the grooved, black surface hides my perennial crop of freckles and this week's smattering of pimples. I fumble through chords on the guitar, matching my *plink*, *plink* to the finger-picking on the record. At last I try the words. "Hush," I say and my voice cracks. I clear my throat and wait till the next line. "Don't," I groan—an inauspicious beginning. Shy of my voice, I stumble through one verse, a scratchy, faint shadow of the singer's perfect notes, but, inexplicably, I'm more confident as the record spins on, and by the last stanza, willingly experiment some, embellishing the melody a bit, trying out a harmony that I have heard a thousand times in my head but never uttered.

Somewhere beyond the drawn curtains of that room lurk girls. I'm dimly aware of this fact and horribly frightened. But right now only the song counts. It protects me. I mumble the lyrics to my picking hand, longing no doubt for love, and stare into the dark hole beneath my fingertips.

Several years later I'm at a beach house, the guitar still planted in my arms. Houses cluster around a small bay, their back porches forming a broken ring around it. Gas lamps and bug lights dangle like Japanese lanterns from poles and scatter a string of identical, rippling moons on the water. It is a bric-a-brac beauty. Guitars and banjos glow and glint, shedding light with the same sort of carelessness as they do sounds. We sing the clichés, songs that *mean* summer, and each face here is a friend—Kathy and Corky and Lumpy and Hank. This is a public singing. Anybody can carry the tune. The guitarists learn it in seconds by watching each other's hands. Familiar choruses, repeated over and over without thought, are really just an excuse for voices to come together, and the simplicity of the melody invites any of the less shy to harmonize. This is concord, affirmation—all that a lullaby is not.

And yet, the moment has a private dimension, too. I sing softly, more aware of my voice as an entity in itself, set off against the others, than as a part of the chorus. I sense an antiphonal quality to the experience that isn't supposed to be there. When I add a harmony line to a tune, I often feel as if I'm inventing my own stage and have this eerie sensation of being very alone and withdrawn that's not much different from the way I felt when I sat in front of the record player and sang by myself. It is the vocal equivalent, I guess, of being alone in a crowd. When the song is over, I lower my head to the soundbox, *plink, plink, plink* softly on a G, and watch the dark spaces on the water below.

Songs register the inner self—and keep a record, too. They recall feelings precisely, in an instant, especially the clumsy first attempts to share those feelings. Later that night I'm on the beach with a girl. She holds the guitar, awkwardly, in her lap and I hold her. I'm trying to show her the fingering to "Homeward Bound"— at least that's my excuse. Her hair keeps blowing in her face, the strands catching on her lips, and when she brushes it back her cheek touches mine. "I wish I was," she sings, "Ho-oh-meward Bound." Later, I hold other girls that way, too. On a very hot night in Virginia Beach I'm showing a different girl how to do chords on the same guitar. She winces, I remember, as she presses down on F, and I laugh. She will be my wife. Now in the shade of a porch beside a Catholic Church in North Carolina, I hold my third child.

"Homeward Bound," of course. Songs remember. I forget songs, but they never forget me. They linger at the edge of consciousness, and, like a familiar face on an airport escalator, pop up at the oddest times, making me smile with recognition, look away embarrassed, and—when it's all over—wince a lot. Not only do they say where I've been, but, like the face that floats by without recognizing me, the songs of my past mark off the distance traveled, too.

I'm fifteen and working as a dishwasher in the kitchen of a deli, my head enveloped in the steam of corned beef that boils in a deep vat beside me. Sometimes this back room gets to a hundred-and-ten degrees and the owner, an ogre in my eyes, doesn't give me a break until the timer in his chilled salad case rings. My Dad, I remember, got me the job and said, when I explained the conditions to him, that I could quit, but I'm in love, of course, this time with a college-age waitress who thinks of me as a nice, younger brother. She slips Cokes my way when the owner isn't looking and watches out for him while I hide in the walk-in refrigerator and cool off among the cheesecakes.

It is the summer of the Rolling Stones and in my memory the song "I Can't Get No Satisfaction," released in a tinny squawk from a transistor radio on the dingy shelves behind the sink, is the continuous soundtrack. I hear it now, see the girl (a wedge of cheesecake in each hand), and reach instinctively for my apron. Instead my hands fall on the lapel of my suit. *I'm* a boss now, not a kid. I *teach* college-age waitresses. The words *no satisfaction* on my lips feel suddenly chilly and record an emotion that marks off the years more accurately than any calendar.

One song—I can't remember its name now—brings with it a hangover. An image of a Ford van flashes across my mind when I hear it on the car radio. I see couples bunched unceremoniously in corners, and the cloying taste of too much Gallo comes, unmistakably, to my mouth. Occasionally I'll be driving (these recollections often hit when I'm in the car) humming a Beatles song like "Yesterday" when a memory strikes, provoked by some phrase in the lyric, and without warning I see my seventeen-year-old hand seventeen years ago opening a blouse on a white, pink-tipped breast. White, I've never seen such white! Suddenly, and contrary to mathematical expectations, I'm not half the man I used to be. My voice fades in and out, trails off in a lullaby whisper. Half of what I ever will be, I pound the steering wheel.

Girls and guitars—I've drifted far from the wasp, the rector's porch, the parking lot, and Sam. Church is letting out. Barbara and the kids spot me. She waves. I still rock Sam and hum "Yesterday." Songs remind me of how far I drift. They are constant, the drone, sturdier than the old house I never get back to and more reliable than the diary I don't keep. At the same time, the songs, so palpable on my lips, promise more than they deliver. It has been a long time, they remind me, since Dad got me a job or, drunk on wine, I huddled with a girl in the back of a Ford van, and I haven't seen a virginal breast in—well, in a long time. "There's a shadow hanging over me," all that "seems so far away," and I'm left with an echo. Matt, my older boy, shouts "hey Dad," lets go of his grandmother's hand, and dashes across the gravel parking lot, tie flapping over his shoulder—all present tense, all now—and I stop humming.

My kids love to sing. It's evening. We are heading back from Grandma's house south and west along I-40 toward our home in Georgia. Around Black Mountain we break into song. Nessa, age eight, starts by setting up a complicated system for choosing what we'll sing. She, naturally, goes first. She takes dancing lessons and likes to sing a song called "My Daddy's Taking Me Out." She rolls her eyes, shakes her finger in the air, and smiles broadly. Barbara tends toward lyrical folk songs like "Where Have All the Flower Gone." Matt—a little embarrassed by all this—usually lets someone else take his turn but does like to sing along. I choose the corny ones: "I've Been Working on the Railroad," "Erie Canal" and "Keep on Truckin', Momma." We're all trying to get somewhere in our songs, it seems. The adults keep the enterprise going. Barbara knows all the words and my job is to hold us to a reasonable approximation of the tune. The older kids, chins perched on the seatback just behind our ears, belt out the parts they know while Sam, gaga, waves his arms mightily and, after a fashion, joins in.

"Row, Row, Row Your Boat" is—groan—my favorite. We sing it as a round, of sorts—meaning that voices can jump in just about anywhere along the way and float "gently down the stream" at whatever pace feels comfortable. Usually we start in the proper, staggered way, Barbara pointing to people so that they know when to enter, but end the song—here's the miracle—at the same time. It's always fun. The kids fall into a heap of laughter in the back seat when it's over, all a-jumble like our voices.

Tonight, somehow, is different. We do the round properly. Voices weave, each alive to the private mystery of its own warbling but joined inexplicably in compact with the group and we end with one voice, my daughter's, chanting "merrily, merrily, merrily, merrily." She finishes confident, but alone, cut free from the flock that has, one by one, fallen into silence around her. "Life is but a dream."

With luck, our songs go beyond us. My father almost never sings, except at parties, but he loves music. He cannot resist beating out a rhythm on the table top when I play a tune. He's great with spoons, too. He was the one who first put a guitar in my hands when I was nine or ten. Several years later we drove to Manny's in New York City, a guitar orchard where instruments dangle from the walls and ceilings to be plucked down by assistants and placed in a boy's lap. I have the guitar he bought there, the only gift from my childhood that I still own.

His mother died before I was born. All I know about her is that she was fiercely loyal to him and played a mandolin exquisitely, at least according to his account. Of course, he thinks *I'm* pretty good, which makes me suspect his judgment, but the way he moves his hand when he talks about her playing convinces me. There's a connection—love of this in him that comes from her—and he sees a dim approximation of it in my clumsy fingerings on the guitar. She *must* have been good.

The thread, I suspect, goes way back, to our primordial beginnings, to that place where songs bring rain and food and calm winds, the time when public and private were one and the voice was not a messenger between the two but the embodiment of their fusion. Something of that sort is being sensed by Dad as he watches the movements of my fingers over the fretboard. I, heading for Asheville into darker mountains, sense it too, as Sam, nearly asleep from his mother's rocking, threads the air with his fingers.

We travel on into the night. Outside, a three-quarters moon floats along the hump-backed horizon. Inside, the dashboard fills my lap with an eerie, blue glow. The older kids are asleep in the back, their piping stilled for the time being. The baby has finally settled down, too. For an hour or so Barbara and I have not spoken, a habit we acquired when we first started driving back at night with babies. We are accustomed to silence along this stretch of road and enjoy, separately, the scene: shades of grey in the mountains' nighttime horizon and towns like nests of light in the valleys. We're nearly home. I think of the log cabin rectory, the statue, the wasp hovering above floorboards, and the pasture wavering in the bright, hot sun. Sometimes silence in the presence of those who know my songs lets me feel the emotions of all songs at once. Unheard melodies *are* sweeter. The baby stirs and Barbara, my thoughts hers, now instinctively sings. "Hush-a-bye," she whispers, "don't you cry," while our car, a nest of chirpers, is hurtled into the dark.

Furnished Rooms

When a room is furnished, comfort is not.
                                                    —Thoreau

I pull into the gravel path and come to a stop, completing the grueling drive from Georgia to Vermont, and my kids race from the backseat of the ladened station wagon to see if, as always, the house key is under the doormat. By the time I reach the door they have already gotten in, checked out the TV, the circular stairway, and the special windows and are jumping on their beds upstairs. I let two suitcases flop down in the middle of the kitchen floor, staking my claim, and find Barbara holding the baby and floating starry-eyed through the downstairs. Above we hear the scampering of the older kids' feet. "The posters," I say. No sooner are the words out than I hear my son's little war whoop and his shout. "Hey Dad! They're here! They're still here!"

All, in fact, is still here.

Consider this small sampling; two wine decanters shaped like ducks, a strand of plastic mistletoe (hung from false, exposed beams in the ceiling), three—no four—lamps made from wine bottles (including one with "punch out" ducks painted on the lamp shade), a small farm scene framed by a horseshoe, and a cutting board shaped like a pig. It's a regular bestiary here. And it's all here, from wall to wall: knickknacks, gimcracks, and trifles. The owner set all this off well: her favorite colors for painting rooms are red, orange, and mustard. She has a weakness for signs to hide the walls, pithy admonitions (all beginning with the word *Notice!*), and clever finds picked up at gift shops like the one that says, in gay 90's script, "Limit five skiers per bed." Clearly everything left over from her attic has found its way to the walls and floors of this house, and, we suspect, every novelty shop in Vermont has been ransacked as well.

And that's just the downstairs! In fact, the upstairs bathroom, the one with the posters, is the real treat. The room is small, five by eight feet probably, with a slanted ceiling that makes it feel even more cramped, but the wallpaper is in a grand, floral design, with stems and leaves and flowers the size of basketballs all over it. When I walk in I think I've been diced and tossed into a garden salad. Above the mirror, glitters a row of lights, the kind clowns have around their make-up mirrors, with a cinquefoil reflector behind each bulb, and on the counter glows a conch shell rigged up to be a night light. There is no bathtub (showers only in the summer) and the shower head is one of those all-in-one types that you find in motels. It has multiple settings with elaborate directions that remain inscrutable to the poor sucker standing in the pulsating stream and sends water-hammer shock waves through the house when it's turned off.

The infamous posters are here. One is a small cartoon of two snails in one shell with the caption "Where did you learn to eat escargot like that!" (This year my ten-year-old son puzzled over that one longer than usual, and I'm waiting for him to ask for a better explanation than the one I gave four years ago.) The other, more memorable one, the one kids ran to see, hangs over the toilet. It is a big cartoon, too, of fifty or sixty naked skiers—it seems as if there is an army of them!—in various poses of gliding, stumbling, and falling downslope, many in, or on the point of, sexual intercourse. Some of the skiers wear swimmers' masks and one, lost under the snow, has on a snorkel. One woman, naked otherwise, has two bobbed toboggans on her bosoms, and talks to a man similarly adorned in the crotch. Another has a surprised look of joy on her face as she has just, according to the tracks of her skis, passed over a low shrub.

"Who would buy this stuff?" we invariably ask. Not us. It's garish and cluttered, "junky" I can hear my boy say, or, as they say in Georgia, "tacky." No one can "live deliberately" in this mess. But we love it. Amid all this novelty we make a path and stack our things. Soon we've set up the playpen and unpacked enough to go to bed. We flop down on matresses not our own, beat but happy, nestled in someone else's world.

Something brings us back every year. This is my fourth and last summer of graduate study in Vermont. We don't have to stay in this house for me to go here. I could choose a place to stay in town or near the lake. Why, I ask myself in November, do I have attacks of dread until we've paid our security money for the next year? Why, I wonder again in May when I forward the balance, do I come back at all?

First of all, there is the circular stairs, a single, metal helix that runs from the living room to the hall on the second floor. To the owner, it's a matter of convenience, apparently—and money. The stairs takes up so little space that the house can have four upstairs bedrooms. At "five skiers per bed" it can house a troop of paying customers. To my kids, though, the stairs is a joy and mystery, a jungle gym and an adventure. After the third day, knotted Tarzan swings dangle from the iron railings and ribbons festoon the pirate's perch. It can be the setting of a storm scene or the stage for spur-of-the-moment romances. They love it; we love it.

"We will never have one of those," Barbara told me after she and I tried to picture what it would look like in our place back home. "We rent there, too, remember?" she said sadly and added, "I don't think they're safe anyway."

She's right, of course. We never would have one, for many reasons, probably. Just as we will never buy a cutting board shaped like a pig. But while here we have it and, in a sense, are released from the oppression of our own tastes and backgrounds. We leave a part of ourselves behind, when we pack up to come, and, for a while at least, feel good about it.

The list of all that we love here is, in fact, long. There's the bay window. It faces on an open field and gives us a different scene each night. Some nights, when I turn out the living room lights, it is all black and gray, the stars visible through the blurry, double-paned glass only after the eyes get used to the dark. Other nights the yard has the appearance of a fairy-tale stage, the field lit white by the moon, the trees a jagged, mysterious black horizon. Once every summer, at the beginning usually, the fireflies are out in such numbers that it seems the stars have tumbled, blinking and guttering in the grass. The next night we look and they are gone, spent on a single, ostentatious summertime display.

And there's the other window, the one with the river in it. For the first three years I propped my chair beside it when I wanted to study, the whispers of the creek drowning out the clatter of a house full of kids. This window was a goad, my conscience and my refuge, and a place to go to get away from books, too. If I closed the cover and shut my eyes, I was in a place without words and heard, as Thoreau put it, "the language which all things and events speak without metaphor, which alone is copious and standard." Now my daughter Nessa has the room and falls asleep at night to that endless jabber, and I'm afraid, when we get her back to Georgia, we won't be able to coax her to sleep without diverting a steam.

My favorite object, though, is a dictionary. I don't know why I love it, really, but I could, I'm afraid, wax rhapsodic on the subject. It's an old Webster's, not unabridged or fancy or particularly fine, just thick. When I hold it in my lap or prop it open on the pillow beside me, I know I have a substantial ally in the war of words. Age and use give this book dignity. There is no crinkle or snap when I open it and turn pages, only an authoritative whoosh. This dictionary has been there. It has seen it all. Several pages are torn, including the one containing words from *palantine* to *palindrome*, but even in that there is comfort. With *paliacious*, *paleface*, and *palette knife* I may have to go it alone, but for most of the rest of the language I have a guide. Every year the book loses a few more of those crescent-shaped index tabs. More pages are dog-eared and torn, and the corners of the cover become more rounded, but the book is always here, faithful and . . . well, I've made the point.

The coffee maker, on the other hand, did not survive last winter—a bad omen. At home, we pride ourselves on the fact that we use an old tin drip coffee maker. It's so *us*, some might say, venerable and wholesome. At the same time we like to make fun of my parents who have a Mr. Coffee. It's so *them*. Glossy and mechanical. So Joe DiMaggio. In this summer house, though, Joe DiMaggio wins and my folks have the last laugh because the coffee maker here is just like theirs. What was so them before has become so us now. My past, in the guise of rented furnishings, is catching up with me at last.

When I see the coffee maker, wrapped in its cord and stashed away forlornly on a shelf in the pantry, a typed warning note taped to the glossy side, I think, again, of my first year at school. Barbara read most of the books for my courses with me that summer. During the afternoons there was plenty of commotion in the house, and we had to carve out some times for a quiet talk. Coffee time was our time. When the kids heard the mechanical gurgle of Mr. Coffee, they could be sure that quiet time was about to be enforced. When they heard the familiar words "Let Mom and Dad have their coffee now," they knew that we were going to talk books and for an hour or so there would be no kick ball or badminton.

In fact, I've grown to love all that is in this house—even the skiers' poster, my comfort on hot afternoons. If I'm reading Dostoyevski and my mood turns grim, the dance of naked skiers is nearby to lift my spirits; when I set aside Shakespeare's comedies to go to the bathroom, I can, happily, ponder this other *Winter's Tale* in my summer place and not lose the comic thread. I may never hang a poster like that in my own house, but if I had not moved my house to where one hung, I would be poorer.

In order to survive the summer we make changes in the place, and in ourselves. In fact, we make many right away. Sofa pillows (old, feather-stuffed ones that spill their insides all over the house and make me wheeze) are taken to the shed even before we unpack. Wooden gates are set up to keep the baby safe, and a downstairs table, used to hold the typewriter, is dismantled so that it can be carried up the narrow stairs to our bedroom. One bed is converted to a change table, and the playpen where the baby sleeps takes up the rest of the room. Within an hour of our arrival, Nessa has converted the porch into a dancing studio and Matt, behind closed doors, does what he can to make his room his own: hiding places are intact, books and assorted weapons have been distributed, and a "keep out" sign is taped to his door.

We seem, in fact, to have come to stay, inventing traditions to cover up our gypsy life, the people this house created in us one summer haunting us the next. Ever since our first year, for instance, when we found a drawer full of soap bars, the kids have done soap carvings. It simply isn't a summer in Vermont for them if they haven't scattered pearly shavings all over the porch.

Another regular event is the failed summer fire. I can't build one. I've studied the problem, watched Vermonters do magic with newspaper, matches, and logs and tried to imitate their ways, but all I get in the bargain is smoke. That doesn't matter; it's a tradition. When the first Vermont cold snap comes, as it invariably does in late July, all gather round to watch Dad try again. The raw material for a good fire is at hand—paper, twigs, kindling, and three logs. I stack it all, construct a teepee of twigs around a knotted page of the *New York Times*, and, ceremoniously, strike the match. Everyone knows the outcome, of course, especially Barbara who is already having a hard time suppressing a laugh. Soon I'm shouting for more kindling, more twigs—no!—more paper, but it's already too late. Nothing works. "Crack windows!" I holler as the house fills with smoke. Well, the kids and Barbara have fun. It's better than the Fourth of July.

In spite of these traditions, though, all of our arrangements are temporary, as most summer ones are, the end never far from sight. You don't keep books on an empty bed and diapers on the bookshelf if you plan to stay any length of time. We live like fugitives. We change some things, but by and large the character of the house remains the same, and any traditions we invent begin with the soap bars and matches someone else left behind. That, in fact, is the lesson this house teaches: we don't create a world of our own from scratch. We make a deal with what is already there.

Nature is comfortable with accommodations like this. Thoreau himself writes about them. "The unanimities of nature in the woods," he calls them, "as when the moss on the trees takes the form of their leaves." Such compromises, he says, account for the "air of domesticity and homeliness" we find even in the "wildest scenes." Put another way, the moss strikes up a deal with the tree.

And any deal in this world is a bargain with the past. One day I took a pen knife and loosened some of the molding in the den of the house. Beneath the god-awful orange walls were the timbers of the original cabin. I pulled away more, investigating where additions were made and walls torn down. The house, I came to decide, began as a two-room cabin, the rest—the kitchen, mudroom, bedrooms, and shed—were added later. What I found, beneath the vulgar imitation of rusticity was a truly rustic Vermont mountain cabin.

I was, of course, appropriately furious. Who in his right mind could have added the orange walls, that bathroom, those posters to this house? The answer, I realized after calming down, was simple: the same person who put the soap in my children's hands. World is superimposed upon world here. That's how life goes on in this summer tale. In one bedroom the original floorboards are partly hidden by an acrylic bearskin rug, and that is completely hidden by the plastic-lined playpen that I drag in. By the time all the generations that live here are finished, the place is pretty junky, a real mess, and I often find myself, on cleaning days, thinking of Thoreau and yearning for a small, Spartan cabin in the woods.

I like the way Thoreau cleaned his cabin. He knew how to take care of a mess! When it was time to clean up, he gathered his belongings—chairs, table, and bed just about did it, I guess—and set them up out in his lawn. No acrylic bearskin rug for him, no plastic-lined playpen. He threw a bucket of water on the empty cabin floor, swept the place clean with a broom and (here's the touch I've always liked most) sat in his furniture outdoors and read until the floor dried. It's a wonderful story. I just don't think it's the truth. I don't believe we ever sweep clean the messes. Not in my summer house and not in our desperate world either. Last week, after I straightened up our place (a matter of rearranging the contents in a fresh and appealing way), I sauntered into the kitchen and stepped on the baby's plastic moose. That's the truth.

"At present our houses are cluttered and defiled," Thoreau writes in *Walden*. A "good housewife would sweep out the greater part into the dust hole, and not leave her morning's work undone." We "have settled down on earth," he adds later, "and forgotten heaven." To enrich the inner life, he suggests, we need to sweep away vulgar conventions—the tawdry hand-me-downs of things and ideas we inherit from the lives of others—and begin anew. "The sun is but a morning star."

That's what he said most of the time. At other times, though, he knew better. "Some interests have got a footing on the earth which I have not made sufficient allowance for," he wrote in his journal. Those "who built these barns" and "cleared the land had some valor." No beginning is pure and innocent, he knew, when he wrote that. In a sense the world is a furnished house—others had a footing here before us—and debts are incurred the moment we set down our suitcases. The morning star and the evening star are one and the same.

We don't start from scratch, and we don't escape without one either. When summer is over, the family and I pack up and try to restore the house to its original, tacky grandeur. The screws I removed are replaced, the table is lugged downstairs, pillows (held at arms' length) are brought in from the shed and set back on the divan, and my boy's hiding places are emptied of their stash.

In the past we've left a few things behind on purpose. Extra food and some stuff from the kitchen cabinet—we'll just leave that, along with a second, worn copy of *The Portrait of a Lady*. The typing table, I'm afraid, may have been dismantled beyond repair; I'm not exactly sure where I put the screws. So its wobbly, battered condition goes to the next renter. Certainly the dictionary, which was used when I got here, is more used now. I've torn at least one page while browsing, and just last week another crescent index tab, this one for *Y-Z*, came off in my hand. I've made my impress there, and if I resist dropping the dictionary in my bags, my thumb smudges will remain to incriminate me. And the coffee pot—we had our share in its demise, I admit, a legacy we'll have to own up to. Maybe one of Matt's drawings can be left behind, as a token of goodwill (and a way of getting back the deposit!). Heck we'll even throw in the citronella. Whoever takes over will need it more than we.

This year will be our last, though, so we'll try to pack as much as we can. Somehow the station wagon that groaned its way from Georgia to Vermont will return with an added burden of badminton rackets and curled-up works of art. We'll find room; the excess is light.

Imagine this: we pack up and head for home, dipping our bodies in motel pool after motel pool along the way, undergoing our ablutions. We arrive at last, beat but happy, in Georgia, and unpack. Out of our luggage come two wine decanters shaped like ducks, a strand of plastic mistletoe, four lamps made out of wine bottles and a cutting board shaped like a pig. "Put that, uh, over there," Barbara says making room, surprised and delighted. Eagerly, the kids follow me back outside. We drag a circular stairs from the back of the station wagon, a dictionary (I couldn't resist after all), and a broken coffee maker wrapped in its cord. The car, we notice, has changed colors, the outside orange, the doors mustard and blue, and there is the sound of a river at one of the windows. And, in the bottom of the last bag, hidden under an acrylic bear rug, is the poster of naked skiers headed downslope, another placard for the mythic billboards of our minds and therefore always our own, though it remains firmly tacked to the red wall we left behind.

The Old Surprises

Flashlight in hand I open the tent flap and unzip the mosquito netting. "Matt," I say, "come see." Walking all night on the beach at Jekyll Island I had found what I was looking for—an excuse to wake my sleeping fourteen-year-old son. The tent is soggy hot. He lifts his tousled head and blinks into the glare.

"Right," he mumbles, reluctantly leaving his dreams and, out of habit, dressing.

We drive down Ga. 50, past the fluttering image of gnarled and dwarfed trees, heading for open beach, Matt eclipsed in a stony silence and me babbling on, giddy from the all-night walk and happy for an audience. "One, two, three, four," I say, poking the dashboard as I speak each number and drawing an imaginary line. "A straight shot across the sky."

"Right," he grumbles.

Pulling into a cabana parking lot, I shut down the motor. We hear ocean crash against beach and see a pre-dawn sky glittering above the glow of the horizon line.

"Venus," Matt says awake now, pointing into dark purple above the dash, "and Jupiter and Mars and the moon—a perfect line up."

Getting out of the car, we head toward the shoreline, shedding shoes and socks along the way. It is the time of the Perseid shower. Meteors scratch the atmosphere, glow momentarily, and die. Sky and water dwarf us. We predict the point of sunrise on the bowed horizon by estimating the widest section of the crescent moon, and, showing the relationships of planetary objects with our fists, feel the heft and tilt of earth against the silent, concentric orbits of a solar system mapped out in the imagination. Our thoughts go out beyond the silhouettes of our hands, but our toes, wetted by surf, cling to the brink of the familiar.

Later we swim, the water oily at dawn as it laps over arms and backs. "Look at this light!" I shout, offering my arms to the eerie day glow. Trees on the shore have turned coral and indigo and our floating faces burn golden.

I crash through the waves to get the camera in the van, but by the time I wade back clouds have rolled in and the magical light is gone. Gone for good, I think, watching clouds heap up on the horizon.

Nothing, though, is gone for good—all comes back disguised in change. The scene rearranges itself, the same story but another time. I am waiting silently in a water blind, this time with *my* father, watching from under the brim of a camouflaged hat as geese in high formation parade across an evening sky.

After a day of kills, cold has seeped into our clothes and boots. Even our silence, riding the steam of our breathing, is cold. We eat Hershey bars for warmth and huddle into our coats, the icy barrels of our rifles between our knees. The waterblind, jerrybuilt out of two-by-fours and plywood and hidden under corn stalks and pine branches, looks out over a calm creek bend.

"Head down," Dad whispers, backing into the blind. He has coaxed some tired birds away from the flock with his call. I hear their dull flapping overhead, a throb like the pounding of flesh.

I glance again, careful not to expose my chin to the keen-eyed geese. There they are—four Canadas, wings set, gliding down. Unsuspecting, the birds coo, listening for Dad's call, their heads bobbing on the stems of their long necks, their bodies turned our way and swaying like globed fruit.

Suddenly—madly—they start flapping. Something has spooked them—one has seen me gawking, maybe, and panicked. Wings flutter, necks crane skyward, they want *out* of here, but all the effort is in vain. The bodies, heavy with earthbound doom, will not be turned.

"Now," Dad says, and we explode out of the blind.

At dusk we head across cornfields to the trailer, flashlights digging beams in the air, our boots crunching frozen stubble. Occasionally a spared corn stalk, betrayed by the light beam, waves its shagginess before us. We carry the claws of the day's kill in our gloved hands, iridescent heads dragging behind us across icy ruts.

The thunder of geese coming in for the night is deafening, thousands of squawking Canadas and snows dropping through a blood dusk sky in long, wavy, casual patterns to the creek—down, down, down—to sleep among decoys of the day's kill.

These vignettes are, in many ways, stories about difference: summer and winter, life and death, dawn and dusk, a man as son and father. Yet, in essentials, they are the same primordial tale, a single story about the beauty and solace of pattern, the whispered call to the other, and the doomed, earthbound heaviness linking and propelling the generations. There is magic in these stories, the urge to imitate by call or photograph, the attempt to claim the earth by naming its delights and imagining its designs. There is also defeat: skyward yearnings, tolerated briefly, inevitably give way to the gentle, but irresistible, downward tug of earth and ocean.

All family stories, if superimposed one upon the other, are the same tale, and this is true, Tolstoy aside, whether the families are happy or sad. When Matt juggles in the living room, the hypnotic rhythm of ball following ball in repeated arcs is both metaphor and reminder. Watching his attention, I yield to the beauty and comfort of repetitions, shedding twenty-five years, my arms grown lighter, my hands quick and sure. Such correlations are inevitable in family life and, in a culture with no traditions except trusty Hershey bar wrappers and reruns of *My Three Sons*, these echoes, these metaphors placing us in this world, are all we have of ourselves in the life before and after us.

What parent has not taken a narcissistic delight in tracing family resemblances in children? My daughter Nessa is the one most like me, a wide, round, butter-and-cream face and a mercurial, expressive nature. Sam, my youngest son and a dedicated thumb-sucker as was I, is outwardly bold and brassy but inwardly has my shyness and those moments of brooding gloominess. Alice, the least like me in appearance—dark instead of blond—has only begun to announce herself, but early indications are that she, too, is one of mine, sleeping with one foot outside the covers as Harveys do.

Matt is more like his mother, intelligent with a powerful and accurate memory. He has not picked up my desultory ways. Like her, he plays to win. Given a goal he will get there, ploughing through distractions with an extraordinary singleness of purpose. "The loneliness of the long-distance runner," I used to joke when as a toddler he would run across a field near our place. It must have looked nearly endless to him, but he never tired, never stopped until he reached the far edge. I think of that now as he swims laps, keeping an accurate toll of their number on a chart; I swim but don't bother to count.

What he has taken from me is the dubious gift of a mind that distrusts answers and broods over questions. "Love the questions," Rilke wrote an aspiring poet; Matt and I are among those condemned to ponder them whether we can love them or not. Introspection is the gift we share.

People have a need, I think, to see themselves in their children like this, enjoying the way sameness persists in difference and the way difference comes to measure how little anything changes. They feel less alone with their idiosyncrasies. I see Matt reach across the gear shift to turn up the radio when a song comes on, and I recognize my high-school self in the gesture. He backs the car out of the drive and I see, in the feigned nonchalance, some of a former me. The more things change, the more they come to look like themselves, and there is comfort in the recognition, as though the minor change of characters in the drama of family life measures something eternal and enduring.

In Lebanon today an Amal boy my son's age sleeps with an Uzi and wakes each morning—each morning like *this* morning—to a prayer rug, a bowl of paste, and a day of killing. He prays to Allah, a fatherly god, but there is no sign of father or family here, the boy's home a gutted, partially roofless apartment, the boy alone. All day he patrols stone-crumbled alleys searching and gunning down the killers of his father and brothers in the hope of resurrecting in the twisted faces of the dead the approval of papa in the smile of God.

Such are the dreadful symmetries, the irresistible designs, that fuel family life.

Like poems, with rhymes that surprise by their oddity and yet ring true, like sex in which difference—ah yes, difference—betrays a shared humanity, our families delight by innovation and comfort by similitude. We dote over a dimple that appears in no family photograph and yet are relieved by the fact that the child, growing up around the dimple, shares our faces and our names. For these likenesses we will kill.

Barbara and I are protective parents. Hovering is our antidote to change, a feeble stay against our children being incorrigibly themselves. Since we moved with Matt, age one, to a remote town in the mountains of Georgia it has been that way. We don't own a television and, when Matt was small, our exposure to the outside world was limited to monthly grocery trips to a small city in North Carolina forty miles away. Until he was four, his world was ours, confined to the glowing circle of our affection and steeped in our language and culture.

That cozy isolation came to an abrupt end when Matt, having attended his first week of day care, marched into the house and announced, to our shocked ears, that he felt ill. "Ma belly hurts," he said in the unmistakable tones of the region, bringing home a new language—one he would have to learn in order to survive in the mountains—and a virus that put us all in bed.

"Where did that come from?" I asked, folding a book over my knee and laughing when Matt made the announcement. Later the grim truth hit. It didn't matter where Matt's phrase came from. What counted was that it didn't come from *us*. This child, with our eyes and face, had acquired a dimple out of nowhere. "The language of your parents is spoken here!" I wanted to declare, as the intrusion of mountain talk increased. No doubt mountain locals feel the same fury when their children bring an alien language home from classes that I teach. This intrusion—this linguistic contagion—is a first clue of the way children, carrying the parental image stamped in the gold of their eternal youth, inevitably slip out of Mom and Dad's loving and greedy hands.

The more things resemble themselves, take on their essential nature, the more, at heart, they change—that is the lesson Matt brought home with his sore stomach.

When Matt was eight or nine he took an inexplicable interest in origami, the art of paper folding. This skill is amazing, and, from my point of view, absolutely amazing because it has nothing to do with his mother or me. I'm pretty good at the basic paper airplane, the folds engraved in my mind after a lifetime of setting rough drafts aloft, but the art of origami bears little resemblance to that inane relief from writer's block. Origami requires a mandarin tolerance for getting lost—a letting go of all will while concentrating on individual, apparently aimless, folds—in the faith that a logic exceeding one's own is taking hold. To me the whole process has the feel of the Christmas Eve nightmare: a million bicycle parts, the damned directions in three languages, and a stiff highball. Only to the patient and plucky—those few who elect to be lost before they are found—does a shape resembling the one in the book emerge.

From my world of all thumbs Matt has inherited nimble fingers. From my dilettantish ways he has extracted patience and single-minded devotion. All of us are puzzled by skills we don't have, but the ones we see in our own children do more than puzzle. They bring us to the edge of chaos and are an affront. "You stop right there," these inexplicable talents say. Observing these innovations, I suspect a devious shaping hand in my life, an atavistic presence, requiring that I live patiently in the folds of my confusion with little more than faith that some solid design, beyond my clumsy grasp, is emerging.

In the golden glow of a Jekyll Island sun my boy—golden too— plays in the waves. I see him, easily within reach, but feel the undertow, enormous oceanic movements, nudging me gently and inexorably, and I see that my illusion of control, of parental continuity, is petty, an irrelevancy in the larger scheme of things. Apparently near as my son and I are, we are being swept along, no different in our struggle to stay afloat than the teenage Amal sinking behind a suddenly pocked slab of concrete.

"The planets are not really lined up," Matt says philosophically, drifting away from me on that golden morning. "They only look that way in *our* sky."

And the sky, of course, is never really ours.

What, I wonder, does my dad see when he looks at me under *his* sky? The image of himself must be hazy, indeed. He supplies the hunting gear each time we head for the gooseblinds, the camouflaged suits that he saunters in with ease. The same clothes smother my stubby, neurasthenic body as I cross the cornfields stumbling in his wake, a scarecrow draped in L. L. Bean. Canadas swirl overhead in great, loosening, broken circles, but the sky is not ours to share, the birds flying at his command, not mine.

Surely when we're in the blind together he discovers in me the limits of himself. Without complaint, he repeats—to this dressed manikin of a hunter who is his son—instructions about the safety and explains, yet again, about aiming ahead of the bird and squeezing through the trigger, aware that at some point these lessons never sink in but aware too that the lessons cannot stop. What, I wonder, does he feel at the command of "now" when he hears me blunder out of the corn cobs and boom away indiscriminately at his sky? What does he feel as the bird honks and turns away unharmed by the heavy artillery of an inept son? Inevitably he shoots down the geese I miss, his limit as well as mine, registering with each shot, I suspect, a pang—the reduction of his presence in a future world. At dusk we lug his bleeding losses to the feather house.

Can I say that Matt has inherited my old love of rock and roll? He has started listening to the radio now, an eerie turn of events because the songs of my generation have made a comeback. It is also eerie because Matt listens for the same reasons I did twenty-five years ago, holing away in the room with the radio to escape family in songs of love and defiance. He listens, just as I did, for garbled messages in lyrics, messages made magical in the garbling. It is for him, as it was for me, the forbidden fruit electrical. In all that, Matt is the boy I was, and yet there is a difference that these recordings, these aural replicas from the past, measure.

In rock, the recording *is* the performance. Anyone who loves a rock song knows this. "Where Did Our Love Go?" is the name of the recording by the Supremes—no substitutes, please. So in the 60's we curled around portable stereos, the changer dropping forever unchanged 45's, or we watched our favorite stars "lip sync" songs on TV—the lips synchronized to perishable tunes that won't die. Like gum, we shared it, and, like gum again, it stays when the flavor is gone. Where *did* our love go, the lyrics ask us now, and what has it come to? The hard truth is that our songs, etched in ageless vinyl, do not restore our young selves even when they boom through our children's speakers. Singing along may be irresistible, but the messages, garbled or otherwise, turn to platitudes on the adult tongue, marking off the distance from a lost past.

"Stop that crying," I caught myself saying to my son once when he was a baby, "or I'll give you something to cry about." The phrase, one that I had hated hearing from my father, appeared magically—a *memento mori*—on my lips. Lost as I may be in the folds of family, I occasionally come across a look in son or daughter, find a phrase or song on my lips, assume a familiar stance in the house I thought *I* had built, and am abruptly made aware that the designs of family life, like 45's in a stack, are endlessly repeatable, but, lamentably, I am not.

When my grandmother was dying, my wife and I flew to her home in Kansas. We brought my youngest daughter—a baby—so that my grandmother, in a lucid moment, could see her, although I doubt that grandmother in her confusion ever focused on her great-granddaughter. Sitting up in bed and wearing a green hospital gown, she was lost in a past that had become immediate. "Hear that?" she said once, "the little stream over there." We all sat silent in the hospital's metallic stillness, the sound of a running toilet in the background, and exchanged glances. In her mind, she bathed in the Solomon River, picnicked with granddad in Colorado, and crossed long, wide fields of winter wheat in the heat of a Kansas summer. To hell with the toilet.

Grandma's dying was hard, as death from cancer usually is. She hadn't truly slept in weeks. She saw beasts coming at her in the night. Awful phantoms that she could not describe stole in windows and hid in corners while her mind raced like a young Amal down the nightmarish corridors of family memory. In her delirium she often mistook the nurses at her bedside for her dead daughter, my mother. I who have my grandmother's eyes and complexion—who share her tendency to nightmares—waited like a stranger at her side, rewarded with atavistic glimpses of my own death. Arriving empty-handed, I had nothing but myself to receive.

As Matt grows into an adult, my size and more like me in gesture and voice, it is clear that there is a core of him that does not belong to me or his mother. At the same time it is clear that there is a pattern here, one we share but do not own. Like the seasons that startle with familiarity, family brings us the old surprises and, unsullied by the nostalgia it generates, measures our lives.

Tics by the pencil sharpener in the hall mark Matt's growth to my height and away from me. He may always see in the mirror a cloudy image of all the old men in his sky, and become them as he becomes himself, but he will soon leave me behind and enter a world that is increasingly his, a world in which he will never be his own man except as I find it harder and harder to recognize myself in him. "Matt," I will say one of those days, collapsing the generations in my delirious dream of stars in line and geese flying low across an evening sky. "Matt, come see!" The stranger by my bedside will lift his head in grief and be my son.

The Garden Wall

Last year it was mulch. I lugged the woods' dead leavings in a wheelbarrow, hugged the loamy mix of soil and bark and rot against my chest, breathing the woodsy musk, spread each load over the shovel-chopped red clay of our gardens and spent the spring consumed by thoughts of mortality. This year it is stone. I'm building a garden wall. My mortarless monument makes its way across the front of our house beneath a bay window and hems in the mulch of last year's garden. Stone by stone it has grown under my hands, changing character as I go: a crude cluster of hardened sinners expanding slowly into a dignified pew of solid citizens.

It changes, too, according to the weather. On clear days the wall sheds its dutiful look, becoming younger and oddly softer in sunlight, glistening like the scrubbed faces of naughty choirboys glancing this way and that. On rainy days it has a monkish air, the jumbled stones a solemn row of cowled heads, bowed or hung or jauntily erect as dignity demands and piety allows. Who knows what thoughts consume them? I'm only half through making the low structure, and already it has redefined our house, rounding off sharp corners so that the place looks less new, and a little more world-weary. Often after spending a long day working there I find myself wasting the evening sitting on the stones, thoughts of mortality arriving again, but in new robes now as darkness seeps into the sloping lawn like the slow advance of mourners and the hum of the woods takes on the heaviness of chapel bells.

There is nothing to building a wall—nothing, that is, except muscle and patience. To get started, I slip on gloves, grab the handle of the plastic cart, and head for the hillside. Sometimes I leave the gloves behind. I like the cart's bump and clank as I walk down the graveled drive, my clatter dissipating into woods and sky as if this were play, though I know full well that the return trip will be all creaks and groans and funereal rumblings.

Along the way I pass a gravesite on a property near ours. River stones, pocked and mossy, sit upright there at the head and foot of graves more than a hundred years old, the whole site of five or six plots marked by orange plastic flags. Surveyors discovered the neglected graves when staking for a house and were forbidden by local laws to proceed with building, the stones of the dead laying claim to the land of the living.

I rarely go past the spot without stopping, paying my respects by standing among the squared-off slabs of river rock. Nothing can be read on the weathered markers, nothing except the simple fact that whatever and whoever happened here ended *here*. Who were they? Poor white immigrants who turned up these boulders when ploughing fields? Runaway slaves who left little trace of their existence except rocks and bones? *Bones*, I think, rattling past. The stones that we carry in us all our lives, stones that rise out of us when we die.

Stones do, in fact, rise. Water collects beneath them and freezes, the ice lifting a new crop to the surface each year. In the mountains the rocks emerge only to be washed downhill by spring rains. They collect about the trunks of trees as if stones, like pups around a bitch, need to huddle about something alive for nourishment. There they remain for the lifetime of the tree—draped in the mulch of a hundred seasons—until the trunk cracks and tumbles and rots, so that the rocks can begin, again, the millennial journey to the creek.

When I get to the site, I leave my cart behind in the road and traipse uphill looking for rocky hiding places. Cold pearls for a warm neck, I think, coming upon stones piled about a beech. One by one I pry them from their ancient settings. I like flat stones, so I only take the ones that lift easily out of the dirt—a simple chore. Inevitably I expose scurrying underlife—slugs, dung beetles, worms, and snakes all snuggling into mud burrows or wriggling into holes. My dream life, I know, has become richer since I started digging, my dark hours haunted by slimy burrowers and centipeded creatures in sectional carapaces. Subterranean spirits at work in the soil are at work in me too.

A stone wall does not require work. It *means* work, as John Jerome puts it in his book *Stone Work*. Agony, I think, is a better word—Greek for struggle, English for pain. In stonework, flesh finds rock, vulnerability meets durability and the result is a scrape and a scar. Like a leaf blown against a chain fence in the rain or a body dragged under a bumper, an inevitable yielding occurs when I brace my legs and lift a stone out of the cart. Under the weight I feel a give in my body opening a passageway to mysteries. Lifting the rock to my shoulder, I think of the hand raised in the cave at Lascaux, dying the calcified interior with life's colors, a hand that later raised stones against the woolly mammoth trapped in a rocky cul-de-sac.

Cherokees who lived here more than a hundred and fifty years ago considered the earth sacred. When they moved a stone, they apologized to the ground. I lift the stones out of their dirt beds with little more than a groan on my lips. Like the rootless teeth of babies, they rise out of the gums of earth where they have lain for an eternity, gray and pocked on one side with lichen, those fingerprint whorls that rocks acquire in the woods, and on the underside brown and red with clay. These I rub with my gloves, raise high in the air, and throw downhill. They tumble and skid to a stop against tree or mound or, running out of steam, pause upright, then tilt into the weeds. In a moment the excitement is over and they are still again, ready, if necessary, to wait out another eternity.

The Cherokees knew about the deadly durability of stone: arrowheads sown into the nearby corn and sorghum fields have *forever* scalloped into each flint shard. Before the Cherokees, the mound builders shaped the earth itself, creating enormous, enduring earthen graves on the landscape. At a spot on the Arkaqua trail, not far from where I live, is a hillside littered with huge, soapstone rocks, gray-black boulders that rise like the backs of dolphins out of the leaf-littered slope. We call the place Track Rock because some of the stones bear the marks of ancient, nameless Indian tribes, marks which by legend are the tracks of fleeing animals. Souvenir hunters have chiseled away chunks of Track Rock and acid rain has pocked the stone surface, but some tracks remain as ghostly, smooth-edged versions of the originals.

"The carvings are of many and various patterns," James Mooney notes in *Myths of the Cherokee*, "some of them resembling human or animal footprints, while others are squares, crosses, circles, 'bird tracks' . . . disposed without any apparent order." When I run my fingers over the indentations, the shapes large and deep enough to hold a hand, I think of the Indian name for the spot, Branded Place, and feel the age-old ambition of humans to lay claim to nature by shaping its stones, the sympathetic magic which insists that the earth and its beasts accept the human imprint, the brand, before the kill.

According to myth, animals left many of these markings on the stones during the great southern migration. Ayasta, the only woman at the beginning of this century privileged to speak in council among the East Cherokees, claimed that the animals at one time suffered famine in the mountains. According to the tale, Grubworm and Woodchuck held council and sent Pigeon in search of food. She flew south and found abundant grain fields, so the animals migrated into the low country—an army of beasts. Mythic hunters had no choice but to follow, accounting for the footprints and handprints in stone. I imagine the circle of Indian faces, streaked with resins, and see skin lit by sputtering fires. I imagine the spears tipped with stone.

Scholarship on Track Rock suggests a more lowly origin; Mooney quoted "sensible Indians" who said that bored hunters chipped out the animal tracks "for their own amusement." Maybe. One of the endearing qualities of the Cherokees is their humor, their willingness to poke fun at their own myths, and maybe the earlier tribe shared this playful spirit. Nevertheless, I am suspicious of the word *sensible*, here, suggesting as it does that the common sense of outsiders can penetrate the uncommon mysteries of another culture. Whether it is true or not, though—whether this is an example of magic beyond our comprehension or America's original graffiti— the ambition to lay claim to forever is the same. Here warm hand met cold stone; the result was a scar.

Stonework can scar more than hands and stone, of course, sometimes taking a toll on machines as well. Several days into the wall project my cart broke down. I had piled in the usual load of stones and, positioned like a donkey at the front, yanked as hard as I could. Nothing budged. When I turned back to check out the problem, I found the cart beached in the dirt, axle to the ground and wheels splayed like flippers on both sides. After I emptied the load and turned over the whole mess, the source of the problem was clear: too many heavy loads had caused the metal bolts to wobble, leaving wide gaps in the plastic, and the chassis had pulled loose from the wheelbase. The cart lies now on my basement workbench, resting in pieces.

I began hauling stones in our car, loading the trunk with rock and driving the short distance from hill to wall, but this led to other casualties. Under the weight of a load of stones, the tires dug trenches in our lawn, and rocks tore at the rubber seals of the trunk, ripping one strip out like an umbilical cord and scratching and denting the metal rim. One rock slipped from my hands, flopped down hill, bounded up a gully, turned on its axis and tumbled—punch drunk—against the bumper of the car.

Yet somehow these rocks, disciplined and chastened into a wall, seem worth the agony, especially at the end of the day when breezes let the sweat dry cool on my neck and five-year-old Alice brings me a beer from the kitchen before dancing off to play with the dog. My stones and I seem like war buddies then—or even better, like illicit lovers, having hugged and grappled with each other only to find that the affair has changed us in different ways, one scrubbed and the other sullied by the experience.

Stone walls have a long shelf life, so I expect these old friends to outlast me, which is an odd comfort. I walk past an old home site nearby, the house long gone, replaced by a new trailer. A hundred feet away, a stone wall—older than trailer, house, or inhabitants—encircles a stump of morning glories and remains intact. I'll go like the stump, I say to myself, walking on. I'll crack at the back and rot from within, leaving Alice to brighten the walls of our making.

Not long ago Dad called, his raspy voice gravelly and somber. His dog, a beloved pet, had died, and he suggested that my family delay a planned visit. My dad is the kind of no-nonsense businessman who uses the word *thing* for whatever is inexplicable. "This thing has really gotten to your mother," he said. "She needs a break."

The dog, a bichon frise that had lived with them for five years and accompanied them on a difficult move from Florida to Kentucky, had been a white froth of energy in their lives when my father's diabetes grew serious and his heartbeat unsteady. All gestures for Dad had become studied and slow, and each one no doubt required just as much effort and concentration from my stepmother, who registered his every move in her mind and heart. Mom cried a lot over the phone. "It's just one of those things," my dad would say.

Now their dog, the one bit of fluff in their lives, had contracted cancer. They kept it alive until the wound was an open sore, a knot of pain, and no anodyne helped. Eventually Mom took the dog to the vet and had it put to sleep. When the vet injected the lethal dose, my mother, holding the dog on the table, screamed and ran from the room, frightening everyone, including herself.

When I got her on the phone her voice sounded subdued, weary, the words sliding away from the ledge of sound like scree shaken loose from a hillside. "Your Dad's taking this real hard," she said. "That dog got him through all those attacks."

Last year my dad had a defibrillator inserted surgically into his chest, a rock-hard device sewn under the skin that clicks in and takes over when his heart stops. The first time it worked he was elated and called in a celebratory mood to tell us the good news—"I guess I would have been a goner without it," he said in a flinty voice—but since then the device has weighed him down. Going off often and regularly, it no longer reassures but serves instead as a reminder of vulnerability.

"We'll get through this thing," Dad says now, if I ask.

"He'll miss his little friend," my mother says, her voice brittle and cracked, and I know suddenly the adamantine silences at the far ledge of love.

Sometimes Alice helps me by lugging stones. Setting her trembling lips and squinting her eyes, she lifts a small rock out of the cart, tottering under her load for a step or two before letting it plop, at last, to the ground. "There!" she says. The rest of the time she leans against the wall or stretches out on the large brown capstone, her body all soft flesh, glowing, evanescent in the sun. She chatters away about butterflies while I pass before her—blue-faced and ladened and leaden. Someday, perhaps, she will build *her* wall while *I* watch.

A stone wall is never just stone: an eye envisions it, a hand shapes it, and a mind holds the boulders in place. Humanity insinuates itself into the ten-ton, gap-toothed smile that crosses an empty field, a monument to flesh and blood as well as bone. Like a poem, a stone wall holds fragility in place, each word mossy on the surface but hard at the core, the whole a solid but serpentine creation of mind and heart. The word *poem* comes, in fact, from an ancient root meaning "one stone piled on another." Plowshares turned up stones and these made their way to the poems that held down the corners of our fields long ago.

So at the end of each day I stand back, exhausted, and admire the poetry of my handiwork. Like books crowded along shelves, the neat rows of chunky and lean volumes yanked one way and another by gaps and crowding, this library of the inarticulate hours bears the imprint of its maker and says all I know about eternity.

It has been my habit each night after finishing a section to pop a beer and sit among my rocky brethren, the cowled fraternity. From my cool seat I look out on the living figures in the evening lawn— grass, flower, cocker, girl. Groundhog, bear, squirrel—and who knows what else—watch silently from the margin. A line of darkness crosses the field, and the tapestry darkens at the edges as woods and nighttime eat into the fabric of the day. My wall is the last to go, the shadows edging up my pant leg before blanketing the stones in gray.

I'm big on commemorations—my meager attempts to hang onto the now—so I've already developed plans for celebrating the wall when it's done. On that evening when I wedge the last stone in place, I will without fanfare conduct my ceremony and pour what's left of the beer over the rocky-hided spirit of my creation. Banishing all thoughts of mortality for the moment, I'll watch soft follow hard, as the liquid trickles down stoney sides. Absorbing nothing and exposing all, the stones hauled by my hands will remain unmoved— my offering of cool, wet pleasures bleeding at length into the black, thirsty mulch below.

Suicide Notes

"I have a desire to create something beautiful," I wrote in a college journal when I was seventeen. I let my hair grow long, wandered downtown late at night, hid poems in my desk, gave recitations aloud in empty school yards, and filled eighty-nine-cent composition books with the usual undergraduate drivel. I found myself drawn like any normal college kid to stark clichés: crows, stubble fields, and winter trees. The poems, empty themselves, were filled with breathless anticipation: "the birds wait, silently, for another note," I wrote in one poem, and in another a girl's "recorder waits, a silent thing." Oh well—waiting *is* a first step.

In writing classes, emptiness continued as the predominant theme, accompanied by Gothic elements: "My nearest shadow, the shadow of my hand, like the shadow your hand makes across the page, is an ancient silhouette." Or: "The trees are black, but like any row of trees hide a white heart." The key to life is hidden somewhere, these poems say, but when we find the secret treasure it is an emptiness we have carried with us for some time. "I like to watch trees against snow," I wrote. "It is as if I hid something there that later I cannot find."

Loss and emptiness—the theme of millions of college poems— was my theme as well, an emptiness that cried out for fulfillment as these clumsy lines from my freshman year make abundantly clear:

> There is something about an empty field
> That makes me want to shout,
> As if a call to loneliness
> Was what I was all about.

Wince. I hope the field *was* empty if I shouted stuff like that! Unfortunately, emptiness was what I was about at seventeen, and I was obsessed with the desire to pour words into the void. More than twenty years later, I'm still at it, and after all that time I think I know why. When I was twelve my mother killed herself with a gun. Her suicide was the blight on my mental landscape and, no matter how loudly I shouted, I could not fill the leafless, crow-haunted stubble field in my heart.

After college I lived in New York with a young wife and took night classes at Columbia, including one in poetry. Eventually—inevitably—the teacher got to Sylvia Plath. My mother and Plath were alike in several ways. Bright, valedictorian types, they were the princesses of their families. Adored by their fathers and adoring of them as well, they married dark-haired men with forceful personalities and had two children. They both committed suicide in their thirties, within a few years of each other.

A difference—for me the difference—is that Plath wrote about her death. For her, suicide was a hobby, a job, and a vocation, and she wrote at length about each of its claims on her. "I guess you could say I've a call"—that's how she put it in one poem. A. Alvarez, a writer and friend of the poet, argues that Plath never intended to kill herself. "The more she wrote about death, the stronger and more fertile her imaginative world became. And this gave her everything to live for." Her suicide was a gamble with the odds "in her favour," but the "calculations went wrong and she lost." All that may be true—she may have died on the verge of liberation from the call of suicide—but it is impossible now to separate the poetry from the myth, and the poems, stunning though they are as literature, at least constitute a suicide note, one authenticated by the mix of despair and abandon that characterizes their tone, by the choice of subject matter, and—regrettably—by her death.

My mother left no messages: no self-dramatizations, no poetry and no suicide note that I know of. There is little mention of problems in her letters, except in occasional denials: "Now I can't see why I was so depressed," she writes in one, "because I have every confidence that things will be back to normal." Most likely, normal was being redefined for her—taking on horrifying qualities that cried out for suicide—but we don't know. The letters are mute.

Did Plath write my mother's suicide note? Brilliant poets tap universal emotions, so in that sense she wrote for all women who had "the call." But, no, that's not what I had in mind at the time when I closed my copy of *Ariel*. The poems emboldened me, but they were not my mother's suicide note. *I* would write that. *That*— I must have decided in some unacknowledged recesses of my mind— is my job.

I've been working on it ever since.

I tried to tell the story first as a novel, describing the final breakdown and the last month or so of my mother's life from the perspective of a boy, named Sammy. Distrustful of feelings I had acquired about the death, I attempted an Ur-novel of sorts, forgetting about plot and consistent character and getting back to the scenes themselves. I retrieved the few remaining luminous mental images I had of my mother—standing in a field in clam diggers, twirling a baton, leaning over the phonograph console, cleaning a window—and attempted to create these, as vividly as possible, in words. The goal was to design a novel built entirely out of impressions—one that did not search out motives, bear explanations of causes and effects, or cast blame. I wanted to bring the past into the present in the way photographs do.

Since I was writing a novel, though, I did have to set the pictures in motion. The result is the prose equivalent of a Super 8 movie: silent, stiff, and a bit unreal:

> Mom . . . looks silly in a sweatshirt and clam diggers, her hair tucked under a cap . . . When the ball comes her way she lets it land, taking a half-step back as if afraid. Only when it dribbles to a stop in the grass does she grab at it with her glove. She bends at the waist, not the knees, in a funny courtly bow and then stands straight again, blinking bewildered. She runs toward us, ball in her outstretched glove, and finally tosses it willy-nilly in the air, looking as if someone had tripped her.

In essence, the story wasn't a novel. I didn't know what to do with my characters because they weren't characters yet but snapshots, bits in a family photo album, and even though this was a story about a violent death it read like a novel in which nothing happened, a hangover from my college poetry.

The boy was a problem, too. When I wrote this book, I didn't know where he fit in, an issue that was as much real life as literary. The boy was onlooker, filter, but—given the agony around him—seemed oddly insulated and detached. I rewrote the story many times but never got that sense of oddity or detachment out of the language. The character was lifeless and, like the college poet he would become, spent a lot of time looking at blank places in the landscape.

> I crouch by the window at the end of my bed, held there by the moon's leaden pull, and look down through bare branches of maple to the open, frost-white yard below. The scene is hemmed in by the heavy darkness of older, woodier lawns—hedges, evergreens, sprawling oaks. Our lawn is the new, exposed center of all this, a drained, colorless, bright clearing.

In a word, emptiness. No matter how many times I rewrote the thing, the boy and his mother—*me* and my *mother*—remained stick figures on (to use a trope from the book) a fixed *terra incognita*.

Years later I rewrote the novel as a series of poems, drawing on the same impressionistic passages, the verbal snapshots, and expanding on them so that they appeared to move in time. I did not bother connecting them into a chronological whole, and I abandoned altogether the pretense of a plot which had always to be tacked on. I merely wanted the characters to come alive briefly—flicker for a few moments as clues to the rest that was to remain unsaid. Now the sense of a disintegrating image was more than self-referential. It began to describe my mother, too, the eerie feel of a life, sifting through my fingers even as I tried to make sense of it, described her predicament as well as mine and forged a bond between me and her, and the—no doubt baffled—reader, too.

In one scene she twirls a baton and I become suddenly aware

that her tentative status as a literary object gives a hint of the fragility of her identity—her sanity—in life. I wrote:

> Her hand—a motion against a motion—blurs and
>   disappears like a detail lost in memory. Her
>   image wavers and fades
> an unsteady reflection
> and suddenly all of her is in danger.

The sense from the novel—that these moments were scenes from home movies—came to dominate the poem, the stiffness of them characterizing her, as well as the poem and me. "I think of some home movie," I wrote,

> . . . each lurch forward riddled with repentances,
>   every wave, pat or hug
> reduced to a nervous tic,
> a caricature. The smile begins
> a moment late and ends before it should, the wave
>   flaring out of nowhere and lingering
> in its afterimage.

"She moves like a cartoon character," I wrote, something created, stylized, vulnerable, and ultimately pathetic, "never losing that hint of disconnectedness in simple gestures and the accompanying sense that something has gone wrong," the flicker of the pages under the thumb serving as a reminder of her detachment from everyday reality both as a created character and as a suicide. On the night of her last breakdown she talks banalities, and her words take on the quality of mine:

> Like balloons around the words in cartoons, her
>   clipped phrases float from her lips in a
>   loose loop,
> drift about the house
> and disintegrate in cracked hoops against
>   chairbacks, railings, and sofa arms.

The poems may have been haunting and odd in the way life becomes for the suicide, but they left something unsaid. Eternally in the present and at the same time forever reminding us of their unreality, they lacked the elegiac ingredient that I needed. The more I worked on them the more I felt I was losing the essence, the part of her I most wanted which was not the disintegrating self, but the self that was disintegrating. This part of her—the person who crumbled—was exactly what I could not name. "She is gone," I wrote:

> Pages spill out of the cartoonists fingers
> and she disappears among the backs of suit jackets
>   and evening dresses and fades behind my
>   clenched eyes
> like a forgotten name.

Near the end of the book of poems, the mother takes the boy shopping in Chicago. They go alone by car on a multilane super highway heading into the city, the beaches (where she eventually killed herself) visible in the window. Oncoming traffic zips past quickly, "a feathery shiver," but cars heading in the same direction bob and float outside the mother's window, "achieving a momentary parity and creating the illusion of stillness."

"Mom floats against all this," I wrote. I had wanted a separate world for her, in my imagination, but the real world, where I needed to place her and my feelings about her, flashed by all in a blur, like the cars.

I tried following a trail of souvenirs back to her. We lived in a 1950s subdivision, and the banality of the objects—the blunt functionality of most of them, the sentimentality of the rest—allowed them to glow oddly once they were isolated and framed in the poem. These were keepsakes, things devoted to who we were, taking me on a journey home.

> Pencils in the house smell like perfume, and erasers, licked hard,
>   are a smooth nut brown.

The magazine rack, its wicker strands curling loose, spills over
with old numbers while new ones—sixty one's and two's—
get thrown away.
In every lamp only one bulb works.
The simplest objects are framed and tinted in the mind: an
ivory elephant with a chipped trunk, beside it a mahogany
one,
the ball bat left out all night on the dewey lawn.
Daily light enters and withdraws from this world; at night it is
backlit, like a dream.

There is an innocence here, the sense that we come upon these
objects fresh, taking them in one by one as if they were someone
else's keepsakes and we were seeing them for the first time, naming
as we go. There is also a searching quality about the passage, the
objects leading us, apparently, deeper into the past, the search mixed
with a voyeuristic sense of doing something wrong, as if we were
snoops or, more accurately, burglars going through a victim's house
with a flashlight.

The list is not metaphorical. It is not one in which each item
carries an emotion. It functions, really, as a series of metonymies in
which emotions are disguised as things, and each object remains first
itself. Reified this way, memory creates, by the suggestiveness of its
ingredients, a hunger for the past that it cannot sate. Composed of
present emotions disguised as objects from the past, the list takes on
a life, but a life of its own. It does not recover the past—nothing
does—but it conveys the nearly palpable sense of loss that inevitably
accompanies remembering the past. "There's more," I wrote,

. . . It never goes away.
A pin glitters in the carpet.
In the bathroom a tie is draped from a lampshade,
the ends neatly lined up as if that's where
it belongs.
And this . . . and more . . . and never enough . . . and
always too much . . .

I was, like most solipsists, seduced by the glossy surfaces of photographs. In photos light played on cheeks just as it had forty years before. Wrinkles, squinting eyes, a curl of hair that flops out of place no matter what she does—all the shagginess that falls away in memory is there in pictures. Photographs, I thought, were my best tools for getting back to the past. I collected them from my grandmother and pasted them into a book. I studied each with a magnifying glass and wrote pages of impressions. My first novel was, in fact, called *Photographs in the Present Tense*.

Inevitably, the more I looked, the more frustrated I became with my position as onlooker: I wanted to intervene. In one section, I wrote:

> My finger slides down the dress front to a pocket sewn into the blouse, a sharp, poofed "v" with a button flap. Cut out of the same material as the dress but tilted against the rest of the pattern, it looks out of place, like a tear in the cloth, and with the tip of my finger I try—foolishly—to right it.

Foolishly because I have been fooled. There is nothing in this picture I can right. A photo—despite its verisimilitude—is not a window to the past because it has no future, no expansion from the moment into choices and possibilities. The picture is an illusion precisely because it is frozen out of time. It gives the "unearthly sense" that we can "reach into the scene and correct, comfort, and control" (as I wrote) and "right" the wrong (as I wrote) because it *is* unearthly, having become, like Keats's still-unravished bride, an image free of earthbound time forever. I wrote:

> The picture's tricks are for the eyes only, not hands which dissolve illusions and resolve another clue into a scattering of dots. My thumb hiding the tip of her two-toned shoe and her dress hem, suddenly comes into focus, freckled, wrinkled, and foolish looking.

Frustrated or not, I filled pages with descriptions of photos, determined with each to have my thousand words. I looked into the glossy surfaces, the way the snowbound longing for rescue gaze into a nighttime window and see little beyond their own image.

I became fascinated with the way songs work as goads to memory. If they are recorded they are like photographs, artifacts from the past that sound the same now as then, but more exciting for the writer in some ways because they have a verbal element to them: they bring back voices. Even when they are not recorded they are verbal souvenirs, allowing us to replicate phrasing as well as words from the past. Writing cannot equal the world it attempts to create, but with songs it can echo it; that was my hope.

I wrote about nights when my Dad was away on trips and my mother played "Fever" by Peggy Lee over and over on the phonograph. For me the song was a talisman and the lyrics worked like conjuring tools, evoking a part of the past that words alone cannot reproduce. When I wrote about the song—hearing Peggy Lee in my head all the while—a flood of associations were immediately available and, it seemed, as concretely present as the tune on my lips. In the novel the boy is in bed, listening to the mother who is downstairs alone.

> I hear the clank of the changer as I draw the twisted sheets up around my shoulders and the long wavering whoosh and whir when needle hits the disc. She turns down the volume but Peggy Lee's voice fills the house to the corners, beating back gathered silences. Clink of ice: swoosh of a magazine dropped to the floor. I scoot lower in my sheets. Snapping fingers, thud of a double bass and a lone, plaintive, female voice. Close my eyes and Mom's there, face lit by the glow of the console. She sways, drink in hand, and sings, watching the record spin, holding the notes out for no one, trying to sound good.

When I heard the song—sung in my head—I could almost hear my mother's voice, overlaying the sound, and so come agonizingly close to the actual sound of her singing. In my mind it is a duet—my mother's voice melded to Peggy Lee's—and when I hear it I've got a bit of her I can claim in no other way.

At least I think I do. I can never be sure. Unfortunately I may be doing all the harmonizing here, reading in the voice, getting Peggy Lee's right but missing my mother's completely. There's no check on that. When I listen to Peggy Lee sing "Fever," my mother is her silent partner after all, my suspect mind supplying the echo, so that the song itself advertises my loss and urges me to fill in. I may have nothing more than the descant to reality with no purchase on the real thing, but it does not feel that way. With these songs, it seems, my mother sings to me.

But no single souvenir, no object, photo, or song was enough, and I became absorbed with more subtle ways of embodying the past. It struck me that my own name—given to me by her—was a clue. It was, after all, the way she called to me when she was alive, her mouth shaping the word each time. I gave the boy character in the novel the name Sammy, one close to my own, and wrote:

> It is all I have to call back her face—my name. My ancient other name. Better than any photograph. Hear it and I see her mouth, the pout of her lower lip on the first syllable, the o-opening of the harsh "a" vowel, the pucker at the "m's," and the final apologetic "y" like the last note of an aria held a moment too long . . .
> "Use two pillows, Sammy," she says, the "y" diminutive and sad, as close to a tear as a sound can be. She lowers herself to the mattress and settles her head with a giddy motion. She pats me awkwardly by throwing one floppy arm behind her, a silly, loving, incompetent gesture. I remember that and her weight beside me and the tug on the blanket as she gropes at it. I see the lit hump of her blanketed shoulder and beyond that the glow by the window where I looked out at the yellow moon above rooftops, and waited for her to call me by my name, my conjurer's tool, the arched eyebrow around which memory constructs a face.

I remember when I wrote the passage being moved by the fact that a name—a mere sound—could bring back something as physical as the weight of my mother in the bed or the inert hump of her shoulder under a blanket. Say the word and shadows coalesced taking on a scratchy, worsted heaviness, and a smooth, breast-warm heaviness, and a sleep-and-booze thickened heaviness. Animated by my breath, her breath rose and fell, it seemed, in the shadows of any curtained dark. The name was a song—an aria, I called it—and when I spoke it, there she was, her face constructed out of a sound on air.

"The poet must conjure the vision of the mother," John Logan writes, "and he must make her sing to him." For Logan, the male poet creates a body of work, a corpus, in an attempt to rebuild the body of the mother. The process begins during weaning when the baby, separated from the mother, begins mouthing speech, thus shaping—with his first attempts at words—the lost breast. Eventually, the poet, longing to give birth to the mother, creates poetry which has as its defining characteristic a "surface of sensual beauty."

Complete fulfillment—one which goes past the lyric and allows for a tragic-comic awareness of life—requires that the poet find words for more than the nurturant qualities of the mother; he must give voice to her sexuality as well, a task which destroys many male poets: "The fact that so many lyric poets die young, or, in Dante's phrase, 'midway through life,' . . . suggests that they cannot duplicate in their work the lower half of the mother's body, the part that *takes*." According to Logan, this re-creation of the lower part of the mother's body—an artistic encounter with sexuality—allows the writer, midway in the journey of his life, to move past a lyrical self-awareness and explore the tragic possibilities of love.

Midway through my life I wrote:

> Sitting at the edge of her bed in her slip, she
>   wads a stocking, points her toe into it, and
>   extends the leg.
> The stocking stretches its length.
> She snaps the hem and picks out or smoothes
>   creases.
> It's a dance routine, a solitary, lavish gesture:
>   calf muscle for a moment flexed, hand
>   habitually and somnolently gentle,

mouth turned upward in a giddy, inexplicable
　　smile,
head tilted.
There is the quietness of it (of hand against
　　hosiery sliding up leg) and the ancient
　　rocking of pelvis as toe finds its full
　　length. She blinks
at this extension—then
shoulder, arms and leg sag.

For Logan, the re-creation of the mother is the poet's metaphorical task, but when the mother is dead, especially when she has
committed suicide, abrogating the body by her own actions, then
the task of re-establishing her physical presence is more formidable,
taking on a literal dimension. In my case, it became a literal re-
creation, something beyond the scope of literature, one which
required constantly frustrated attempts to reify her presence, to
make her happen again.

I wrote and I wrote and I wrote—for what? Snippets of songs,
a name spoken in the dark, and a few curled "word" photos. I
attempted to fashion in words a replica of her life and chiseled,
instead, a grave marker. A flash in the dark. The hard lesson of all
this writing is that words do not make up the loss. An ode to spring
does not melt winter snow, and suicide notes, no matter how
contrived, do not revive the dead. Suicide, I had come to learn, *is* a
photograph—a luminous instant cut off from the past and dead to
the future, and the future included me. But I didn't stop. I wrote
and wrote and wrote—I'm still writing, shouting in an empty field
of blank pages, my hunger sharpened by my cries.

Midway through life I had to kill my mother. I tried, as Sylvia
Plath tried with her father, to put a stake in the fat, black heart, and
rid myself of this ghost that was never fully alive as a presence and
never going away, either. So, I wrote about the shooting, trying to
get past poses to the blunt fact of her death. It is, after all, the only
fact I know for sure:

She stops to tug at a loose lock of hair (the one that always falls on her forehead) and scoots in front of the rear-view mirror to fix it. A glimpse of the end of time, an appropriation of the future in an instant—that's suicide. Like a wedding photo it's posed, intended for a dignified spot on the mantel.

She can't be thinking of the truth—of the way she will look after the shot, the gore that makes some poor bather step back. She can't be thinking . . . no, it is the framed view in the car mirror she sees as she purses her lips and tucks back loose hair—a final pose that she intends to pass down, a pose but for the holding held forever, and in deference to the intention, I see it. I do. I hold it in words and acknowledge that I see it for as long as I can—I do.

But she takes a breath, and the pose, as poses do, gives away more than intended. It is a pretty snapshot creased by worried hands. And I who keep the picture for a lifetime must face the other truth: the gob of flesh splattering the back of a driver's seat, two quick and ugly involuntary jerks, blood pumping and sucking a gash, a lock of hair that tumbles out of place no matter what she does, and the idiot eyes rolled back, and back some more.

There is more than this, thank God, much more, but it has nothing to do with words. It is, instead, a matter of death and life.

It begins with a photograph, another frozen image, but does not end there. In this photo my mother, age six, stands beside a toy airplane. The side of my grandparents' house stretches behind her and—up in the corner—the legs of a boy perched on the porch rail dangle, casting zig-zag shadows on the shingles. In the bottom corner, in my grandmother's wobbly hand, is my mother's name, Roberta, in blue ink. The wall is pocked, here and there, with white bubbles—some defect in the photograph—and the whole picture, printed on cheap paper, has faded to a light sepia tint. In fifty years the image will fade completely, leaving nothing but her name on a glossy blank.

The airplane looks like an elaborate scooter, a boxy replica of a flying tiger with a wooden prop, exposed engine cylinders, three rubber wheels, and a tail with an official looking ID number stenciled on the side. Who knows how many kids it went through before it found its way, battered, to the back of some garage and eventually to the Glen Elder dump?

My mother, the six-year-old, stands in the center of all this, leaning casually—well, a *little* stiff, I guess—against the stubby wing of the plane. She wears a knit top, pleated skirt, stockings and a pair of Mary Janes. She's decked with a feathered, turban-cap, the kind fashionable in the 1920s. She wears bangs, just visible under the short brim of her cap, and has a tentative smile on her round face. It looks as if the camera clicked a little too soon or too late. Shadows fill up one corner, but there is no sense making too much of them. They are cast, no doubt, by some large, friendly tree in the yard. Anyway, there is nothing ominous about the picture at all.

"Look," my wife said one morning when our youngest daughter, Alice, played in the living room. "Doesn't she look like pictures of your mother?"

Alice and my mother share a round face, brown wispy hair, olive skin, an impish smile that curls only at the corners, dark eyes, and a habit of looking down, coyly, when they smile. The resemblance is striking. When Barbara spoke, I thought right away of the photo of my mother beside the airplane. My impish daughter Alice can be found in the photo of my mother, I thought later when I dug the picture out of the album. I showed it to Alice, telling her that it was of her grandmother when she was Alice's age. Alice looked and giggled, her mouth curling at the corners like the mouth of the girl in the picture. "Oh!" she said before scampering off, delighted and full of herself, my future and my past. The photo tipped from my fingers and fell onto the countertop. Alice, I realized, is as much of my mother as I will ever know, no photo and no poem, but a real live girl.

Art has no answer for death. It is a temporary balm encouraging us to go on. Words, even in our poetry, do not recapture the past—nothing can—and they correct nothing. All they can do is bring the present to bear on it, demanding a response now and in time. It is a call to live, but it is not life itself and never can be. But, if our words are beggars, new life puts a penny in the palm and the humped, shadowy figure retreats clutching the coin. New life is the only answer to death, and I say that knowing full well that death inevitably has the last word.

My older daughter, Nessa, was born on April 6, the date my mother died. The coincidence has, I think, always been symbolic to my family and (despite the obvious pain of remembrance it brought my grandmother) a solace—and lesson—to all. I don't write about my mother much any more. The photo albums have been put away and are rarely subjected to the scrutiny of a magnifying glass. My subject, now, is my family, the living one. The symbol of Nessa's birth was one of the first clues that the answer to this childhood death lay not in the past but in the present and the future.

The shift in emphasis can be seen in the last revision of my Ur-novel. I used a frame story, placing horrifying events of my childhood against the life of an adult narrator who, like me, now has a family of his own. While I was writing this version, Nessa, who was around six or seven at the time, was performing in a dance show which required a sequined outfit, bright red make-up, and a baton. Pleased by her commanding presence in such a bizarre get up, I took a picture of her. She stood in the driveway holding her baton in the air like a queen.

I thought, as I brought her orange gaudiness into focus, of the line I had written about my mother's twirling—her face a "flickering of after-images" behind the baton—and saw Nessa standing brazenly behind hers, smiling, brassy, glittering, rouged, and full of life. Not long afterwards, I wrote (yes, wrote, what else could I do!) the ending of my novel. It is, I suspect, the best way to end this suicide note, as well.

Nessa skips on ahead, kicking up gravel as she goes. The afternoon sun turns her hair golden and streaks the skirt red. I wish I had a camera, I think, but quickly correct myself. A camera can't catch a dream, and Nessa looks like a dream come true—not the dead dream of a photograph but a dream with a future.

I look at the spring field ahead of us and imagine it in midsummer, ladened with life. These dry stalks will be gone then, beaten down by rains, roots pulled loose from damp soil.

Tall summer grasses will take their place, green and brown with blue woven in. Queen Anne's lace, tall, heavy-headed weeds with a black petal curled at the blossom's heart, will pose in the bright still summer light. Crickets and grasshoppers will buzz and snap everywhere. Nessa, in this probable future, will race through waist-high grasses getting burrs and beggar's-lice on her skirts. A new puppy—something domestic and golden and floppy, a cocker maybe—will trail behind and then dart ahead barking shrilly.

By now Nessa, stepping out of the dream and back into my life, is way ahead of me. Her arms, outstretched and flipping beside her, toss planks of light into the blue day. Midway down the path through the field—without warning—she does a cartwheel, her legs cutting a vaguely calibrated arc in the air like a baton flipped deftly and spinning just out of reach.

Monogamy

She waves and breaks into a happy run, the whole of her tossing quilted colors on the air. She wears blue-jean shorts with a little cuff at the knee—a skinned knee—and a sailor's cap pulled down over a shock of sunlit hair. A T-shirt flaps against the curves of her body. If she were a little girl, she would leap into my arms but she's not—she's nineteen—so she stops short, pats me on the chest just under the collar, and, bending at the knees, laughs.

"Guess what!" she says, and then tells me the news. Who knows what it is: an A on a test, a phone call from a boy, an acceptance letter from a school? None of that matters now, except her, the fact of her. She stands before me, and we share the planet for a moment—a planet that tilts her like a gem in the light. How could I not take joy in her every time she stepped my way?

Oh, I understand the psychological dynamics of this sort of thing. I'm over forty. She was born twenty-two years after me, within a week of my graduation from college and a month and a day after I got married. The year I started teaching she entered kindergarten. The feelings I have for her are associated with a longing for my lost youth and are, I know, a mask for the fear of my contracted possibilities. My life is a house, doors shutting behind me as I walk through, and now that I'm passing by the room with her bright window in it I hesitate to go on, fearing the click of that door behind me as well.

What strikes me—grips me—is the force of these emotions, their power to consume my otherwise sensible self. The platitudes of rock-and-roll seem profound, and my prose goes greeting-card

117

soft. Long drives are necessary but do no good. I pick things up—
quarters, pencils, leaves—hold them briefly to feel their solidity or
scruffiness, their reality against my palm, and then open the fingers
wide and just let go.

These feelings lay dormant until graduation time. I played my
usual distant and avuncular self when she was my student and spent
a long time simply trying to recognize what I was feeling. I remember one night we stood beside my car talking about nothing, about
school. Classes hadn't started yet, and she had time to kill but no
excuse to stay. Finally there was a lull in the talk. Moonlight sifted
through the elms like chalk, powdering her arms and hair. Luna
moths played around the streetlamp and katydids went crazy in the
grass. Near the library we could hear the laughter of students, the
call of her world, not mine, floating down the hill beyond us.

She glanced in that direction, about to push herself away from
the car, and, at the thought of her leaving, I suddenly felt bereft.
"So, what are you taking this quarter?" I said idiotically. I already
knew her schedule as well as my own, but the maneuver worked,
earning me another two minutes with her. She ticked off classes and
hours on her fingers, and I watched as the planet tilted her again,
this time toward its lesser light. This is crazy, I remember thinking
afterwards as I drove off, windows down on the car, the air blowing
past me in a dizzying, exhilarating rush.

I introduced her to some books, works by Plato, for instance,
and Kate Chopin and Lao Tzu. She took all to heart and mastered
them. When she had a bad night or picked up a poor grade she
sometimes came by and cried in the office until I could tease her
back to smiles. I talked her through a breakup with one boyfriend
and listened with delight to giddy stories as another boy drifted into
her life. I showed her *Daisy Miller*, though I didn't need to. She *is*
Daisy Miller, and the book was hers to give to me.

I noticed all that is girlish about her: the whine that worked its
way into her voice when she turned ironic, the white of her scalp
which showed when she pulled back her hair, her legs—long,
athletic, a little lanky—which she folded under her when she sat, the
freckles cast along her arms like pennies in a fountain, the skinned
knee. In time, though, I saw what at first I had missed: the s-shaped

tug that worked into the zipper of her jeans, the sharp turn of her ankles just above the canvas tops of sneakers, the long, slender, tapering fingers of her hands—hints of the woman she had become.

I do not envy her boyfriends—that is the innovation here and a clue that these emotions are not easily pigeonholed. When I see her grab her boyfriend's neck in the dining hall and kiss his hair, I'm pleased by her passions. I want all that for her. She needs a boy, several boys, who will discover the world along with her, not some father figure like me. And yet when we talk I see the beauty of her neck as she looks up and off and my response is not simply paternal. I have to check my hand.

A few days before she left she said good-bye at the gazebo on our campus, and the vague feelings I had for her coalesced, became suddenly as unmistakable as they were ambiguous, and hit me like the knowledge of death. She wanted to thank me for the year and looked away, mumbling "you just don't know." The talk was hard going, and I kept up my end with inanities. I probably asked her what she was taking next fall at the university—no doubt I did.

Finally we got to the boyfriend she had left. I like him very much. He is intelligent, carefree, and simple in his loves. Her leaving hurt and baffled him at once. For months he would show up on campus slumped on porches or under trees like a sack of beans, letting stones and leaves sift through *his* fingers. She spent several months putting up with his long looks and teary eyes, complaining that he followed her around at parties, turning maudlin. She wanted to know why he would not just leave her alone.

"You are a treasure," I said, "and he knows what he's lost." She looked at me. "A treasure," I repeated. She glanced down and when she looked up again she was fighting back tears. We talked a little more, and I remember she tried to say good-bye but couldn't. She gave me a quick hug and ran off, wiping her eyelashes and hiding her face so I couldn't see her cry. By Sunday she was gone, and I woke up the next morning thinking about her. All day I heard doors click behind me.

A part of me—a thoroughly American side attracted to fresh starts and destruction—says do the unthinkable and go for her, sacrifice all for the chase, ply her with sweet words which are all I have, and "give her boyfriends a run." But that is not how I feel about her. It is not how I ever felt about her. I cannot even invent the scene. She would wear a baggy T-shirt, probably, and white shorts—no, jeans—and her hair would be wild and mussy, as usual. She'd have on those goofy, child-pastel sunglasses but take them off when she stepped into . . . into *what*? She would . . . no, I would . . . oh, *it* would. . . .

The page slips through my fingers and rides a lazy, see-saw arc to the floor. The scene has almost no shape in my mind, and whatever shape it assumes turns comic, pathetic, or banal—a violation of the rush of undefinable emotions I do have for her.

One problem, of course, is that she wouldn't have me. A middle-aged teacher would be a terrible mistake for someone who smiles most of the time, cheers with her sorority, and kisses her boyfriend on the neck after class. To her all of this interest on my part would be merely weird. There are other considerations, too—my children, my job. But beyond these simple matters of life and death is an obstacle that dwarfs the rest: I love my wife.

I love Barbara more now than when we first married some twenty years ago. I love her in volleyball shorts, the thighs tapering to a pinch just above the knees. I love the way my shirts hang on her when she works the garden. I love her skin, milky on Saturday mornings in bed. I love to watch her stand on the porch wearing blue jeans and a yellow tank top, and I love, too, the look on her face when she closes one eye and sinks a set shot from the edge of the driveway.

Our love may not move the sun and moon, but it has a history, the adventure of living mixed in. The eyes I kiss—once the bills and laundry and dishes have been shoved aside—have read countless terrible poems by my hand, and the ears I search out with my lips suffered through the songs I wrote and sang back when I wrote and sang songs. Barbara knew me before I knew poetry or bird species. She knew me before I read *Ulysses* or had the who/whom distinction down cold. She kissed me awake on the day my first poem was published and held the hand of my dying grandmother. She knew me before I was me and largely shaped who I am.

Barbara is, without apology, a nurturer. She does not, as Virginia Woolf puts it, see herself in relation to reality except as she stands in relation to others. She does not have, nor does she seem to want, a room of her own, though she often looks out others' windows and rarely complains of the view. In all this she is my teacher—the teacher's teacher—giving a dreamer like me lessons in how to live in a family. "Why don't you take pictures with people in them?" she asked when we first got a camera and I snapped "artistic" photos of mountains, creeks, and storefronts. "Get at least *one* kid in every shot!" Ever since she has been putting kids in the picture for me.

If I handed her shoes to put on the baby she invariably gave one back and pointed to the baby's foot. When I let a baby fall off the change table, she slapped me on the back and said "it could happen to anyone," not letting me off the hook for incompetence. I am among the paternity-disabled but an eager student so the lessons continue. "Get baseball cards," Barbara whispered in my ear last week when Sam came down with the chicken pox on the Fourth of July. Why didn't *I* think of that? Without her I would float through this family like an idea—a mere word—and would have, in the end, missed all. She grounds me in us, where I belong. With her, word is made flesh.

Fourteen years ago, on the night that my first daughter was born, Barbara and I skirted crescent beaches on the road to the hospital—doing eighty. We passed a lake alive with borrowed light. The pre-dawn glow of cabins on the shore, an anchor lamp, the incandescent moon—all burned a taller, darker twin on water. Headbeams gouged a way into the dark, separate moons on an asphalt horizon, and—fanning a concrete slab—faded in the hospital carport's neon dawn.

In the delivery room, three candy stripers leaned against a wall and observed over the doctor's shoulder. "This is the easy part," Barbara said to the girls, her face dark red and mapped with veins. She had at last reached the stage when she was allowed to push— and did, as hard as she could. One by one, the candy stripers—all youth under their pink masks—slid down the wall and fainted on the floor. None of them saw the doctor put the blood-prize in

Barbara's lap, a mystery reserved for those who had left youth behind.

I recall, too, a time when Matt, my oldest son, was reborn before our eyes. At the age of seven he had to submit to anesthesia, and Barbara and I were told to hold him on the table as he came out from under the drug. We watched his faculties return: the limbs moved slowly, as if under water, and the breathing changed from a somnolent monotone to deep gulps after air. The death mask of his face, expressionless and dopey under his mother's kisses and his father's steady gaze, assumed the animation of intelligence. He opened eyes, glazed with unconsciousness, and held one arm out between us, moving his fingers like an infant. "Look," Barbara said, holding now his cheek, now his hand as they came to life, each part of his body filling with purpose as a room at dawn grows familiar in the light. "Oh, look!" With our hands on the awakening flesh of our boy, we saw seven years of maturation recapitulated in moments, and felt the majesty of the life our sharing had created.

Unfortunately, marriage, "with its orgasms estimated in the thousands," as one writer put it, is hardly the stuff of lyric poetry. In memory, the passions of monogamy (that low groan of a word) tend toward the generic. Where, after countless nights of lovemaking, does sex fall in the memories of husbands and wives, memories so easily displaced by freshly gratified desires?

I remember our first bedroom in a place called The Barn Apartments—pine walls and red curtains. When sunlight filtered in, the room took on a woodsy, autumnal glow, a tinted cellophane beauty bathing us in crimson. Sometimes, in the midst of morning lovemaking, we'd find ourselves just looking at the halo on our skin—our fingers passing through spirit on the way to flesh—and we'd laugh at our iridescence before being swept up by passions which carried the glow to our core.

This was sex at home, our first home. In fact, sex at home is one of the simple, sweet facts of matrimony, which mercifully stops the ugly business of sleeping over at a lover's apartment where one, at least, is not "at home." Sheets take on a soft familiarity when they are "ours," and beds have deeper pockets when sex there is followed by sleep. Lovers rendezvous, assigning themselves to any hastily agreed upon hideaway, but husbands and wives at the point of ecstasy share a home-coming.

We moved to New York, a city so congested it crowded out the weather and drove us into each other's arms. Our building rose some fifteen floors from the concrete of Broadway but remained dwarfed by larger highrises on every side. All we saw from our windows were washed-out stucco walls illuminated by reflected light. When Barbara's body emerged in bed above mine, sheets falling away, it seemed to disappear among the beiges, and I watched the only colors in the room: the splash of red at lips and breasts and the bit of sky—our only sky—in her eyes. All that year our weather happened indoors.

We lived briefly at Martha's Vineyard in a bay-front bungalow with a loft. These were single digs, the kind reserved for wealthy bachelors and steamy, summer romances, but we had the place for the off-season and invaded with our conventional lives of long books and long, long walks. We learned to name birds together that year and tramped over sand dunes with their wavy fringes of sea oats, binoculars in hand, adding ocean birds to our lists. Night or day we could make our way to the loft, no kids to slow us down. Outside the seabirds—heron, tern, and gull—passed by the window offering their monotonous squawks, while our cries, so human and expressive of our shared momentary delight, rang out and dissipated against the swellings of the sea. That year Barbara conceived our first child.

Since then, we have enjoyed the game of having sex with kids around. What, I wonder, is better than my wife's body in my arms on a Saturday morning with the sound track of a Ninja Turtle video filtering through the walls? She turns to me, all sheets and skin, the light of white walls a cool mother-of-pearl, and runs a finger down my spine. "Heroes," she whispers, "in a half shell."

There is the love scene that hasn't happened yet, but I can imagine it, and the picture does not turn comic, pathetic, or banal. All the children but Alice, our youngest, are gone, and she's a high-school senior off on her graduation trip. With the kids away, Barbara feels a little blue so I take a blanket off of the bed, grab a bottle of Chianti, and prepare the tree house which like our bodies was built for kids but made for love. I set out candles, the guitar, pillows—the works—and invite her for a walk. When we arrive she gets the picture.

"You jerk," she says—ever the romantic—but before she can protest I've already unbuttoned her blouse. The cat follows us—a new one, I guess—and old Agee, our Argos, is able to hobble down and settle into the leaves at the base of our tree. In the woods, rabbit, coon, and muskrat curl into knots of fur. A pair of barn owls flutters by and perches in a tree across the creek. Leaves glitter. How wonderful and odd and white and happy are our naked bodies among all this! Even the moon—that voyeur—cannot resist and watches by the light it stole for us.

If I had to pick one time, it would be an autumn morning when Barbara and I were young parents in our late twenties. What is better than lovemaking in the morning, the sunlight giving skin its stubbornly opaque textures and lusciously translucent colors? Barbara looked particularly radiant that fall, having trimmed down after the birth of our daughter though her breasts were still large and roseate. I ran my hand under them, tickling her a bit. Deeply veined and luminous, they felt hotter than the rest of her and appeared animated from some source beyond us, the springtime of our lives, *our* youth, here to be squandered daily in nursing. I leaned toward her, tasting the salt in the hollow of her collarbone, and she reached for the headboard, not laughing now, not solemn either, but lost in all that we spend our bodies on. When I held her tight, milk leaked on my chest and mingled with our sweat in the perfect emblem of marital love.

At graduation, I made my way through the usual sea of black gowns. Eventually I found the student I was looking for and slipped her a note, but we immediately floated apart—drawn away by the tide of the crowd. The note read:

Words are never enough—that's one of the themes of literature—and I felt the full force of that hard truth the other day in the gazebo when we tried to say good-bye. I'm more than half in love with you—you know that—and, if I were not a very happily married man, I'd give your boyfriends a run. I like your freckles and your skinned knee. Don't grow up too quickly.

Why do we do such things—make such declarations at the risk of being made the fool? Maybe it is a way to say good-bye, but I doubt it because the note was written more to me than to her. It is my flirtation with who I am not, an announcement of this giddy infatuation with what I simply will not be. It, like this essay, indulges the moment to destroy it, the writer, I suppose, growing up just quickly enough.

Drifting in the graduation crowd, I tried to see her one more time while undergoing the customary post-graduation ordeal of shaking hands, giving hugs, and posing for pictures. When I did find her, she was walking toward me, looking bedraggled, but happy, in her loose gown, the open note in her hand. She reached over my shoulder with her arm to give me a hug and kissed my cheek. At last she said good-bye. I am best for her when I am a teacher, guiding her through the world I know and wishing her well in a world that does not include me—that is the truth I came to as she disappeared in a swirl of black robes.

After the graduation crowd had dispersed and it was time to go, I drove off (what cliché should I use?—my head spinning? a lump in my throat?), carrying the present moment like a torn envelope in my lap. When I got home, Barbara—my love past and future, the love I can name—stood in the driveway looking beautiful in jeans and a yellow tank top, shooting baskets with our son.

The Geometry of Lilies

Flowers can bloom from the mathematical mind. Matt, the mathematician in the family, wrings petals from paper by practicing origami, the ancient, Oriental art of paper folding. Given enough paper and time, he can create a garden of intricate shapes. It is the complexity of origami that drives him—a hundred folds for a single design is not uncommon—but what he does has its own grace, a thumb-twisted elegance. The result is a wondrous mix of clarity and clutter, a paper knot in the form of a rose, perhaps, or a daisy, a creation that seems light and whimsical, the intricacy relegated to accordion folds hidden away.

Matt wadded up a lot of paper in his early attempts at the art. He found a book on the subject—a bad translation from the Korean with sentences like this: "Through the occlusion of fold 'a' angles 'b' and 'c' emerge simultaneously." Little emerged from such language, unfortunately, and even when the instructions were clear, the task remained complex and difficult. The simplest shape required ten to twelve folds any one of which, done wrong, turned up a donkey with two tails or a three-legged giraffe, mutants which found their way, in a wad, to my son's trash can.

With practice Matt learned most of what he needed to know and eventually mastered the subtleties of the art. In minutes now he can turn a sheet of colored paper into a flower, a donkey, or a star. No flat page in the house is safe. A quick inspection of one shelf turns up a dog, a swan, a camel, a grasshopper, a pig, and a panda. Pterodactyls, wings clipped snugly to the next shelf up, hover menacingly above the scene. I love to watch him amid such clutter create designs, his fingers producing abundantly within the constraints of his own devising. Love and discipline meet in these shapes, a boundless, creative energy in the mix. I see in them a rough draft for the geometry of lilies and catch a glimpse of the folds in our lives as well.

"There's something to keep you busy for the next twenty-one years," my brother-in-law said folding back the baby's blanket when Matt was born. Barbara—the new mother—and I looked at each other, dumbstruck, but after a night in which both of us had walked the crying baby we knew he was right. Something had changed. Until that time our lives had seemed one long Sunday afternoon, the only imposition on romantic bliss an enormous lab-collie that scratched the door on rainy nights. Now a baby!

It was not the work that worried me. An eager volunteer, I charged into dribbled breakfasts of strained peas, limped through afternoons hauling a tot on my hip, and dragged my feet all night over a square of carpet in the nursery, flopping in bed at dawn, a weary veteran, tired but okay. I could deal with drudgery, but the lost spontaneity ate at my soul. In my memory I see Barbara taping a calendar to the refrigerator the day we brought Matt home. I bet the hospital supplied it. From now on we live according to a schedule—that was the message sent with our folded bundle.

We're not talking about a big loss here. Barbara and I were not flower children, but we did at times just take off, telling no one. I remember before Matt was born, going to the pancake house at midnight on a whim and eating a big breakfast. Barbara was in her ninth month, then, and I should have realized when she waddled with me to the checkout that changes were on the way. I didn't. "No dust upon the furniture of love": it could have been our motto. Two weeks later when the source of Barbara's waddle slept in my lap, we ate pancakes at home and turned in by ten.

We devised escape plans, of course, like everyone, hiring baby sitters and imposing on grandparents in order to slip away and taste the old freedom, but such wanderlust required planning, jottings on the calendar, groveling phone calls, and haggling over money. Moments away became precious, not to be squandered on the casual or frivolous; they were big events with maps, and grandma waving good-bye from the porch, and suitcases thrown in the back of the station wagon. Such occasions required haute cuisine. Sadly, I haven't had a midnight breakfast at the pancake house since.

And what does the poetry between the lines of our calendar say now?

Monday:	Alice (gym) 3:30
	Elementary (Alice) 6:30
	Soccer 5:30
	Band Boosters
Tuesday:	Soccer 4:30 S & A
	5:30 Nessa
	EVERYONE! 4:00
Wednesday:	PICTURE DAY!
	Dr. Revell 10:30 Alice
	Marcia's 7:30
	Body Shop!
Thursday:	(Sam) Elementary 7:00
	Hum Workshop
	Lynne's 6:00
Friday:	Elementary 11:00
	Body Shop!
	3:45 (Sam)
Saturday:	Franklin's brunch
	Matt Magazine Sale Key Club Party!
	Body Shop!
	Dinner Dale
	Soccer Game 4:00
Sunday:	To Tennessee!

Ah, Sunday. Ah Tennessee! Leave soccer and PTA and gym behind. That's the wish. Leave behind the Hum Workshop and Dr. Revell and Alice (gym) and (Sam) elementary. Strike out for the territory. Go and *go*! Go west, to *Tennessee*! The phrase may be nothing more than another bit on the calendar, one more place where two or more must gather at least in name, and (Alice) and

Sam no matter the wishes of Mom and (Dad) come too and the receipt from Dr. Revell tucked in Barbara's purse and the soccer ball lolling about in the back of the mini-van and the mini-van newly undented for now. They all come and more, with new fillings and PICTURES! and, of course, EVERYONE! (the auditory delights of the Hum Workshop still ringing in their ears), these and a clarinet and flute and all the exclamation points we wanted to use (but hesitated), these come, too. Come and *go*. Go west! To *Tennessee*!

Sometimes in the folds of my calendar days I recall—with neither fondness nor regret—my last fling. It was spring break, a few months before my wedding, and several of us concocted a trip to Florida. The goal was a little peach-colored cinderblock house somewhere in Dade county. I could go, I was told by my friends. In fact, I could drive. Barbara stayed behind.

We were an odd assortment, the embodiment of the American dream, I later came to see as this trip took on mythic dimensions. We had a Lumbee Indian with us and a pretty blonde with porcelain-white skin. There were others too, in other cars. We were young, headed for the tropics, and giddy with freedom.

I don't remember much of the actual stay in the pink beach house. All night we huddled together in the living room sitting cross-legged on a circular scrap rug, passionately dissolute, drinking and singing songs. Sometimes a joint was passed around the circle. Sleeping consisted of crawling off to some corner, alone or with someone else, and passing out in our clothes. By day we found ourselves, somehow, on the beaches going through the motions of an ocean holiday which included a good deal of prone sun worship and burial in sand. The temperature of air and water and body were all nearly the same and we floated through endless liquid afternoons, animals living in the mere present, perfectly suited to our world. I recall my delight in being able to walk into the front yard and pick an orange from a tree!

What I remember most, though, was the trip back in the car. We sped along I-95, driving at night when it was cooler, a silhouetted backdrop of palms and palmettos darkening the west and, to the east, the ocean spreading beside us, a moonlit runway to adventure.

Miles of orchards lined the highway, the globed fruit dotting dark trees with a thousand temptations far into the long night. We stopped to steal oranges from a grove only to discover—after we were back in the car and safely down the road—that they were, much to our disappointment, grapefruit.

Somewhere in Florida, the sun rose. Palm trees, backlit by ocean, crisscrossed the sky in a striking imbroglio of glitter and darkness. Dawn light filled the car, illuminating cut-off denims, a long blond thigh, and a brown arm flopping across a pastel blouse, the couple asleep in a tangle in the back seat among pillows, suitcases, boxes, and guitars. As dawn light filled the car, their bodies began to take shape in the rear-view. Cherubic faces. Closed eyes. Tousled hair. In the coppery glow, I could see that they were holding hands, the fingers interlaced. Suddenly hungry for home, I looked past the mirror, ahead at the open road, a straight and endless trail of tolls.

Under the glow of a desk lamp, triangles give way to other paper shapes as Matt makes new creases, each one folded on the table and set in air between thumb and forefinger. At some point the folds become interlocking, like a knot, held by the integrity of the shape rather than the sharpness of the crease, and another lesson sinks in at the fingertips.

It is hard to see the final design of one of these gestating creatures until it is too late. Until, that is, the final shape is inevitable. Eventually something forms, a red bird in this case. It rests on my palm, dead and still to be sure, but animated by the tensile energy of its folds, the mixture of care and grace hidden in the cavities of its twisted breast. It is hard to resist the temptation to open folds and take a peek—find the secret of this little miracle.

The secret isn't in the creases, though. What, after all, are they? I open the design and spread the page out on the kitchen table, a web of lines. Spine disappears among ribs and the heart—which is the shaping, not the shape—has gone out of it all.

When the heart goes out of it all, I'm at the crossing, parked in a vacant lot by an anonymous intersection in the middle of nowhere.

Two stars rise in clouds beyond the windshield. Two points. The shortest distance. Clean and uncomplicated. The geometry of desire brings me here. A woman walks up, her footsteps resonating among the clatter of dripping trees. She has black hair, say, and long legs, her skin a sea of milk. She stops—the night stops—and she stoops by the passenger window, tilting her head in greeting, her hair spangled by rainwater. I stretch across the seat and let her in. A rush of perfume floats ahead of her into the cab—the stab of the illicit— but she sits like a little girl, leaning against the door and looking into her lap. I pat the seat closer to me. When she slides over, I put my hand on her knee and . . .

. . . the dream scene shifts, a freckled knee now under my palm, and the day a sun-drenched hillside dotted with daisies and clover and dappled lawn stretching behind the woman down to a stoney creek. She squints at me across the quilt, her mouth hesitating just shy of a smile, and looks away again quickly at some warm sunlit square between us, her fingers playing carelessly with the fabric fold, her red hair a blaze of afternoon orange, a color I have never seen in life. I lower my head so that my eyes can engage hers, my look a question. Are you sure? She nods again, looks up at me . . .

. . . and bites her lip. A birthmark runs down the inside of her thigh, a small dragon shape just above the knee. In the marquis-lit motel room, where all this that never happened happened easily enough, bed and woman look unreal—sheets and long blonde hair swirled in some dreamy confection. I'm unreal, too, some joke of myself standing there in underwear and T-shirt, in a room of commonplace day dreams, where little in fact seems real, but . . .

. . . the dragon, and when she bends her knee, oh, *does* it seem real, releasing me from the origami of my calendar life with one deep groan.

"It's dumb to stake your life on something like that," Barbara says, snapping the black head of a spent day lily from its stem. To make the earth say beans—that was Thoreau's goal. Barbara thinks the earth should sing and the tune should be day lilies.

Fluted, thick-lipped and heavily veined, the day lily bloom rises to the dawn. Straining for light, this garish imitation of the true lily, peaks by mid-morning, its cheeks following the sun to an apex in the long summer sky. By late afternoon it begins to flag, the heavy head drooping at sundown and blackening with night. Many days Barbara walks the garden snapping dead-heads and pulling up desiccated stalks. She's right of course. All these pretty colors. It *is* dumb to stake your life on something like that.

She sets the plants in fall. It doesn't take much—a shallow trough and a sprinkling of dirt over the tuber. She's no avid gardener, but it is common in the evenings to find her standing in the garden squinting at what's left of the sun, her jeans mudstained at the knees, her gloveless hands brown with dirt, the veins at her temple and wrists blue from stooping. When I come on the scene dressed in a tie and jacket for work, she smiles sheepishly and invariably brushes loose hair back from her forehead, leaving a brown streak. Sometimes, acting coy, she threatens to give me a muddy hug. Such are the requirements of the geometry of lilies.

I'm the first one up in our house, usually. I grope downstairs in the dark and sit alone in all the quiet I can muster. It is the delicious time when silence fills with the clicking of the house and the rustle of loved ones clutching pillows and turning away into the dark. All settles into a quiet made thick and sweet by subtle violations: creaking footsteps, distant cars. Soon morning takes the duskiness out of windows and the mechanical aubade begins. Clocks sound off, one after another, faraway alarms that lose all urgency in the distance and become, like any faraway noise, a song not of ourselves. The interlocking music of other spheres. A love song.

Such is the geometry of lilies.

Barbara has brown hair—not blonde or black or red—and she wears it simply, pulled back some days by a tortoiseshell clip. I remember my joy when we first got married at finding hair clips in my sock drawer. We are after all what we take for granted and what we misplace gives us away. The ribbon in with the pencils makes us real.

Such are the requirements of the geometry of lilies.

"If your trade is with the Celestial Empire," Thoreau writes, "then some small counting house on the coast . . . will be fixture enough." The shack at 2000 Pacific was not, I suspect, what he had in mind, though the building was plenty small and what happened there accounted for much of my future dealings with the universe—celestial and otherwise.

I had come to the place in Virginia Beach by accident at the end of my freshman year. Not really by accident, I guess, though all that was lovely that summer had the authority of the accidental about it. I came harboring some elaborate scheme for meeting a girl I had seen at school that year, a dark-haired ingenue with big eyes and a habit of tugging at the cuffs of her blouses in a way that, somehow, endeared her to me. I was, I suspect, ripe for love.

The only place I could find to live was a tiny, two-room frame house with an enormous sign announcing the address: 2000 Pacific. A waitress in the local donut shop/restaurant/bar helped me go through the newspaper looking for possibilities. She also poured coffee, cracked jokes, found two roommates for me, and made fun of my laboriously carefree pose: sunglasses, cut-off jeans, and ratty loafers. When I got discouraged about finding an apartment, the waitress pulled my glasses over my nose comically or popped me on the side of the head until I cheered up. She found dimes for my phone calls, poured more coffee for free, and slipped extra donuts to me when the manager wasn't looking. The waitress, of course, was Barbara.

Soon I forgot all about the ingenue. She didn't arrive until midsummer anyway, looking a little pathetic in a white waitress uniform with smudged cuffs. By then I didn't care.

All of us that summer worked indoor day jobs. Barbara used her influence to get me installed in the backroom as a dishwasher. My roommates took jobs as hotel janitors. We worked long hours, fueled by summer love, and walked home from our jobs pastey white but proud among bronzed vacationers. When it got hot—and it did get sheet-sticking hot daily—we went to the local convenience store, the Slurpy an excuse to stand in the air conditioning.

It was easy under the guiding lights of the celestial empire of that summer to fall in love. Above us the stars swirled like dust tossed to the wind in a moment's caprice and set in the sky for a lifetime. At our feet waves crossed each other and in the ripples, back eddies, and rills churned a shape of endless intricacy, a design repeated in the eroding hillside, the splayed branches of the elm, and later in the whorl of my son's own fingerprints. The intricacies these share is the geometry of lilies.

Nights when Barbara and I walked the beach we held hands, a parody of the old couple we might one day become. We followed the slow, jetty-fractured curve of the coastline where water, crashing against breakers with all the force of the heavens, spends itself in a white rush, carves cozy places in sand and languishes in pools. On those summer nights the planets lined up for us without our knowing (which is just as well), and the impulse to flee a family and the inevitability of becoming enmeshed in one met when we held hands. The celestial empire spread above us in the sky and reflected before us in water, found an outpost on earth in the counting houses of our hearts, the folds of Matt's graceful designs implicit in the splash of stars, the crossing of waves, and the easy interlacing of our fingers.

Geometry was the only kind of math I could do in school. Picture math. I liked to fill a notebook with drawings that looked like spilled Tinkertoys. The language of geometry claimed my attention as well. Cuts, intersections, vectors, angles—the vocabulary of new directions, the vocabulary of change. There were circles, of course, pure and wholesome pies, but these waited helplessly on the page, ready to be cut into slices by some shortest distance between two points.

In geometry, one becomes two with a slit of the pencil and two become many at the slice of an angle. Given enough intersections, the pie begins to look more like the calendar on the refrigerator than a math problem—more like the mess of our lives. When it reaches that point geometry alone probably cannot handle the tangle.

But math has gotten shaggier recently and its students have begun taking clutter seriously. What, they ask, *is* the structure of a mess? They study fractals, the building blocks of irregular edges, and wonder at shorelines or leaf-shapes or riverbeds. They take on the whole universe with a word that best describes my life—*chaos*—and study the way things pile up and overflow, embracing all that is baggy and rumpled. They try origami, the art of knotted paper, and, alas, consider the lily, aware that complexity has a hidden elegance. Accumulation—the junk of our lives—has a loveliness we are just beginning to understand.

This faith in life's messes is nothing new. Even the austere Thoreau could not resist the ragged edge that forms when man and nature meet. "Simplify!" he exclaimed, but secretly he admired the messy cuts railroads made through hillsides. "Few phenomena gave me more delight than to observe the forms which thawing sand and clay assume in flowing down the sides of a deep cut." What struck him was the way such a flow imitated other forms in nature, the churn of ocean currents, say, or the fluted splurge of vegetation. These shapes may be "grotesque," Thoreau writes, the world's "excrements," he admits, but he finds in the mess—in the apparent randomness of this flow—a common creative gesture, a unifying force. "You find thus in the very sands an anticipation of the vegetable leaf," he says, and adds: "No wonder the earth expresses itself outwardly in leaves, it so labors with the idea inwardly."

There is nothing mechanical in the way nature repeats itself, though—not according to Thoreau. "Simplify, simplify," is *not* the way of God who like all artists creates by metaphor: "with excess of energy strewing his fresh designs about." The creases in nature sink deep, but the fold is on the oblique, the shapes spinning out from the center by surprising analogies, not symmetries, the unity—the elegance—in the shaping, not the shape.

And so . . .

The weekend says Tennessee and carries a crumpled dentist bill in its pocket.

The earth sings lily and traces the blue veins of Barbara's wrist on a petal.

The tangle of arms—coppery, aglow—in the dreamy rearview mirror says go home, *be* home.

The thigh says dragon.

And the blank sheet of paper says fold—this way and that—the shape of your life emerging in your hands.

Such is the geometry of lilies.

Epilogue

Barbara and the kids bought a Cross pen for my birthday present last year, an act of faith, they suggested, knowing my record for losing pens. How do I lose so many? A word or phrase comes to me on the bus or in a park and I stop to jot it down. Pleased with myself, I neatly fold the piece of paper, carefully tuck it in the pocket above my heart, and walk on, leaving the pen behind on seatback or ledge, a donnée for some other writer, I suppose.

I'll keep this one always, I promised the family, and I did, diligently for a month, before the pen followed the others into oblivion by falling down a drain in Atlanta.

It has been a season of losses for our family. In a sense we have been grieving all year in anticipation of our oldest son going to college. How many pens have I lost along the way as he dashed through the pages of our lives? Once I wrote that he would become himself as he grew older and resembled his father and grandfathers in his life—suggesting a linking of the generations—but that is only half true because I see now that he will take whatever he is far away and leave us with as much of ourselves as we can stand.

What can I give him as a souvenir? Perhaps I'll return his gift, give him a pen, too, a little something for him to lose.

Other losses have been more serious.

Last month my dad died. He had been ill for years but the death, on the heels of the death of my wife's father two months earlier, was a blow. Dad had taken a turn for the worse two weeks before he died, and I was there for his last weekend. I arrived at the tail end of visiting hours, I remember, and rushed to the intensive care unit on the fourth floor to see him. He was on his side, his face gaunt, his breathing ragged, the jagged line on the monitor overhead keeping up with the bad news.

I startled him and thought at first that he didn't recognize me, but that wasn't true. He watched for a long time—just watched my face and held my hand. "I've got something to tell you," he said at last, and then he began a series of messages, one for my brother, another for my wife. He mentioned each of the kids. "Tell them I love them all," he said.

The nurse came in—it was time for me to go—but Dad waved away the oxygen mask. "Tell me about your book." So I did, explaining that after twenty years of writing, yes, it was true, a publisher was interested in a book of mine.

"Too bad I won't get to see it," Dad said, gripping my hand. I tried to tell him that it was a book of essays, not a novel or anything exciting. No big deal, I told him, but he was ignoring me, his mind on the truth.

"I'm convinced," he said when I stopped blathering on, "that there are reasons for these things." He stopped talking, and the nurse fitted the plastic mask over his nose and mouth.

Most of the time that weekend I simply sat with Dad, holding his bluish hand and making small talk. All the chit-chat eventually got to him and he asked me—as politely as he could—to stop talking until I had something to say. I had brought my guitar and hoped to play softly for him, but the rules about noise were strict. "You'll never get it past the receptionist," my stepmother said when I showed her the guitar case, and she was probably right. So, much of our last days together were spent in short stints of near silence every two hours. Dad's sluggish pulse thudding under my hand.

The last story I told Dad during my chatty phase was my solution to the pen problem. "I just buy a new pen on the sly," I told him. I keep a stash of change in the bureau, and everytime I lose a pen I cash it in and buy another. "Cross pens are all alike," I say, "so no one notices."

Dad laughed. Then he coughed and spat in a cup. That's when I saw his point, and cut back on the small talk.

I only hope, in this year of losses, that he was right about the meaning of things—that nothing just happens and that there are reasons for our disappointments. "That's what my book is about," I wish I had thought to tell him, "the hidden laws of our simple lives," but in my numbed state I wasn't thinking. "Maybe God knew I had one more chapter to write," I say now to console myself as the book goes from my hands into the hands of strangers.

After spending the weekend with Dad, I drove back to Georgia and an empty house—all the family gone on errands or out to dinner. When the house is empty I like to play my guitar and sing—loud. So I strapped it on and let out the tensions of the weekend by bellowing a tune and banging on the strings. Halfway through one song a string snapped and unraveled with an awkward, cartoonlike *boing*, and I suddenly stopped, the house silent around me. A few hours later folks from Kentucky phoned to say that Dad was dead. Though I had the itch to play and sing loud, there were no strings in the house and the guitar—the one Dad had given to me—remained mute.

There are, perhaps, reasons for our disappointments.

Later that night Matt and I drove together into town—I had to pick up some beer—and on the way I tried to say something to my son about my father and dignity. I described the various ugly procedures performed on his body. At one point the nurse ran a tube as long as her arm up his nose to flush phlegm out of his system causing Dad's whole, beaten body to rise in bed and writhe. I told Matt that his grandfather suffered this and other indignities to the flesh but didn't complain. "It's a battle, son," Dad told me the day he died, as I left his bedside for the last time, and I told Matt that I wish I had had the sense to say to him: "Dad, you're fighting it well, with dignity."

It was dark in the car, but Matt was driving and on the word *dignity* I realized, for the first time, that I would write an epilogue about Dad for the book. The thought came to me, like that, the way these thoughts do. I reached for my pen to jot down the word *dignity*, patted the shirt pocket twice, and smiled. The pen wasn't there.